AMAZING
WORLD
ATLAS

lonely planet
Kids

CONTENTS

AROUND THE WORLD

AROUND THE WORLD (CONTINUED)

QUIZ & INDEX

How to Use This Book

The *Amazing World Atlas* makes it easy to find the information you want.

These two pages will show you how it all works. Main entries begin with one of the seven continents: North America, South America, Europe, Asia, Africa, Oceania, and Antarctica, in that order. Following each continental entry are pages devoted to regions and countries within that continent.

If you want to know about a specific region or country, you can look it up in the index.

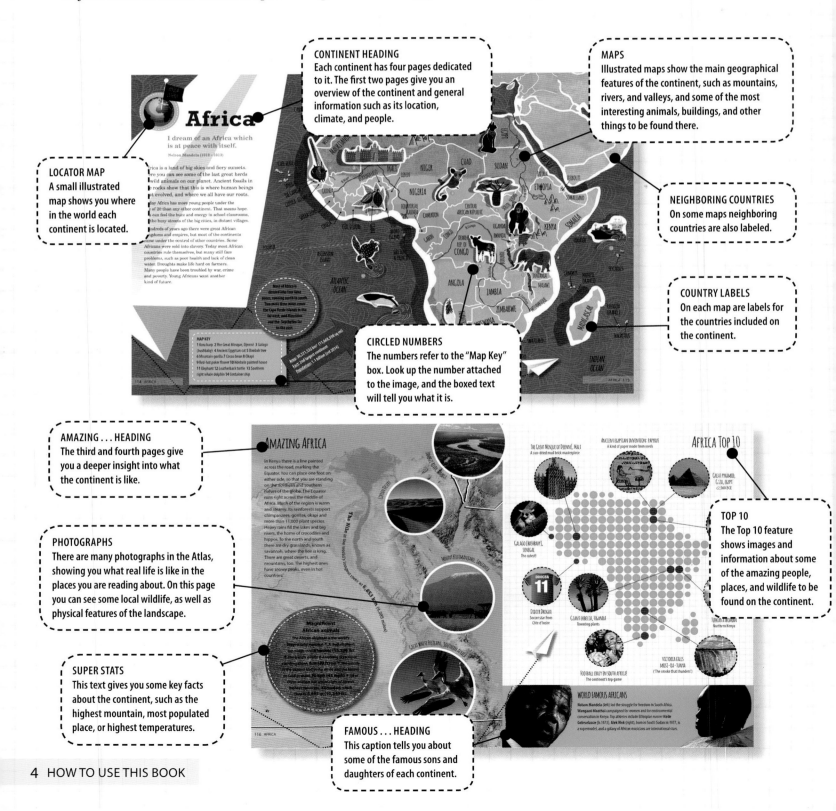

CONTINENT HEADING
Each continent has four pages dedicated to it. The first two pages give you an overview of the continent and general information such as its location, climate, and people.

MAPS
Illustrated maps show the main geographical features of the continent, such as mountains, rivers, and valleys, and some of the most interesting animals, buildings, and other things to be found there.

LOCATOR MAP
A small illustrated map shows you where in the world each continent is located.

NEIGHBORING COUNTRIES
On some maps neighboring countries are also labeled.

COUNTRY LABELS
On each map are labels for the countries included on the continent.

CIRCLED NUMBERS
The numbers refer to the "Map Key" box. Look up the number attached to the image, and the boxed text will tell you what it is.

AMAZING ... HEADING
The third and fourth pages give you a deeper insight into what the continent is like.

TOP 10
The Top 10 feature shows images and information about some of the amazing people, places, and wildlife to be found on the continent.

PHOTOGRAPHS
There are many photographs in the Atlas, showing you what real life is like in the places you are reading about. On this page you can see some local wildlife, as well as physical features of the landscape.

SUPER STATS
This text gives you some key facts about the continent, such as the highest mountain, most populated place, or highest temperatures.

FAMOUS ... HEADING
This caption tells you about some of the famous sons and daughters of each continent.

REGIONAL HEADING
Continental entries are followed by regional entries. These give more detail about the various countries and regions within the continent. Most regional entries cover four pages and, like the continental entries, the first two give you an overview of the country or region, and the third and fourth provide more detail.

MAP
The map illustrates the region covered and labels the countries or states included.

CAPTIONS
Captions give information about real life, culture and history, valuable resources, statistics, or landmarks found in the region.

ENTRY HEADING
This heading tells you which part of the continent (countries and/or regions) the entry covers and, where necessary, lists the countries or states included.

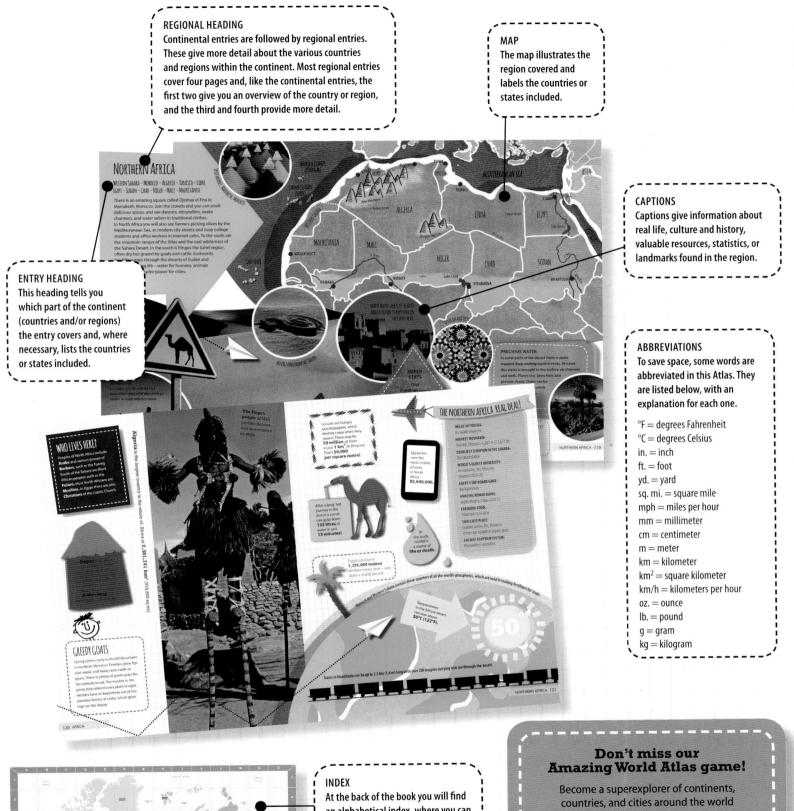

ABBREVIATIONS
To save space, some words are abbreviated in this Atlas. They are listed below, with an explanation for each one.

°F = degrees Fahrenheit
°C = degrees Celsius
in. = inch
ft. = foot
yd. = yard
sq. mi. = square mile
mph = miles per hour
mm = millimeter
cm = centimeter
m = meter
km = kilometer
km^2 = square kilometer
km/h = kilometers per hour
oz. = ounce
lb. = pound
g = gram
kg = kilogram

INDEX
At the back of the book you will find an alphabetical index, where you can look to see if a particular place is covered in the Atlas. The numbers following each index entry refer to page numbers.

There are also grid references that refer to the world map at the beginning of the index. These numbers and letters are in normal type.

EXAMPLE:

Don't miss our Amazing World Atlas game!

Become a superexplorer of continents, countries, and cities around the world

✳

Test and grow your geographical knowledge with interactive maps and games

✳

Discover fun facts about sights, wildlife, food, and culture

✳

Challenge your friends and family

Download it today!
Search for Amazing World Atlas in the iOS App Store and on Google Play

For more information visit **lonelyplanetkids.com**

Planet Earth in Space

Our planet, Earth, is one of eight that orbit the Sun. It is the only one we know of that can support life, though the quest continues to find others.

The Sun is one of many stars in our galaxy, but it's the only one we can see during the day because of its size and the heat it exudes. At its center the Sun's temperature is about 27,000,000°F (15,000,000°C). And it measures more than 620,000 mi. (1,000,000 km) across its diameter. It's so big that a million Earths could fit inside it!

The surface of Earth is very young compared with that of some of the other planets. That is because it has changed a lot since it was first formed. Movement below the surface, such as earthquakes and erosion by water, reshapes it over time. More than two-thirds of Earth is covered in water. Ours is the only planet on which liquid water can exist, and water is essential for life.

The oceans also help keep the temperature stable, another factor that is important for life. They are aided in this by the carbon dioxide in our atmosphere, which traps warm air. This is known as the "greenhouse effect."

Phases of the Moon

Old moon

Half moon (last quarter)

Waning moon

Full moon

Waxing moon

Half moon (first quarter)

Crescent moon

New moon (invisible)

The light of the Moon is actually light from the Sun, which reflects off the Moon's surface. As the **Moon orbits Earth**, we on Earth see this reflected light at varying angles. That's why the shape of the Moon appears to us to change. It takes about **29 days** for the Moon to orbit Earth, cycling through all the phases and arriving at the beginning again.

Our Unknown World

Up until the 20th century, we had no complete maps of the planet. Then we began to be able to take pictures of Earth from space. This allowed us to fill the gaps in our knowledge of the world. **Pictures from space** also help us predict the weather and are especially useful in showing where hurricanes and other storms are going. Earth seen from space is a beautiful sight. It's mostly blue because of all the water on its surface, and it's often known as **"the blue planet."**

Neptune

Neptune is the eighth planet from the Sun and the fourth largest. It's a gas planet with a rocky core. Its rings are dark, but we don't yet know what they're made of. Neptune has the fastest winds in the solar system, sometimes reaching up to 1,242 mi. (2,000 km) per hour!

Uranus

Uranus is the seventh planet from the Sun and the third largest. It is a gas planet with a solid metal core. Its blue color is caused by methane gas clouds, which block out red light. Uranus's rings are dark and made of large objects up to 33 ft. (10 m) across.

Solar System Data

	Mercury	Venus	Earth	Mars	Jupiter	Saturn	Uranus	Neptune
Highest Surface Temperature	806°F	896°F	136°F	23°F	−234°F	−288°F	−357°F	−353°F
Lowest Surface Temperature	−292°F	896°F	−129°F	−125°F	−234°F	−288°F	−357°F	−353°F
Diameter	3,032 mi.	7,521 mi.	7,918 mi.	4,212 mi.	86,881 mi.	72,367 mi.	31,518 mi.	30,599 mi.
Distance from Sun	36 million mi.	67 million mi.	93 million mi.	142 million mi.	483 million mi.	0.9 billion mi.	1.8 billion mi.	2.8 billion mi.
Length of Day	59 Earth days	243 Earth days	1 Earth day (24 hours)	1 Earth day	10 Earth hours	10.7 Earth hours	17 Earth hours	16 Earth hours
Length of Year (orbit around the sun)	88 Earth days	225 Earth days	365 Earth days	687 Earth days	4,333 Earth days	29 Earth years	84 Earth years	165 Earth years
Orbit Speed	105,946 mph	78,339 mph	66,622 mph	53,859 mph	29,206 mph	21,562 mph	15,209 mph	12,158 mph
Confirmed moons	0	0	1	2	50	53	27	13

Our Solar System

Saturn
Saturn is the sixth-closest planet to the Sun and the second largest. It is a gas planet and has a solid core. Saturn is famous for its stunning rings. They are mostly ice but may also contain pieces of rock. The smallest particles are about a half an inch (1 cm) across.

Jupiter
Jupiter is the fifth-closest planet to the Sun and twice the size of all the other planets combined. It looks solid, but what you can see are actually clouds. Jupiter is a gas planet, probably with a solid core about the size of Earth. Its rings are difficult to see.

Mars
Mars is the fourth-closest planet to the Sun and the seventh largest. Mars has many interesting geographical features, including the largest mountain in the solar system, Olympus Mons, 15 mi. (24 km) above ground level.

Earth
Earth is the third-closest planet to the Sun and the fifth largest. It's small and rocky, with many different geographical features, such as mountains, evergreen forests, rain forests, plains, deserts, valleys, and, of course, oceans!

Venus
Venus is the second-closest planet to the Sun and the sixth largest. Like Earth, Venus is small and rocky and it probably once had water, but the high temperatures on the planet boiled it away. There are many active volcanoes on Venus.

Mercury
Mercury is the closest planet to the Sun and the smallest. It is rocky, with many of craters.

Sun

Time Zones

Different places around the world have different clock times, or time zones. This is because, in addition orbiting the Sun, our planet spins around on its own axis.

The axis runs north to south, from pole to pole. When the part of Earth that you are living on is facing the Sun, it's daytime. When it's facing away from the Sun, it's nighttime. Different parts of the world face the Sun at different times as Earth spins. So if we want noon, or "midday," to happen at more or less the middle of the day, we have to divide the world into different time zones.

For this reason, if you lived in Barcelona, Spain, and got up at 8 A.M. and decided to call a friend in New York, they may not be all that happy because it would be only 2 A.M. there. New York's 8 A.M. happens six hours later, when it's 2 P.M. in Barcelona. Those six hours are the difference between the two time zones. Think that's complicated? Some countries have time zones of 15 or 30 minutes' difference from the next zone along, rather than a whole hour. And some, including the U.S. and most of Canada, also have "daylight saving time," when people alter their clocks at certain times of the year to make the most of the light hours . . .

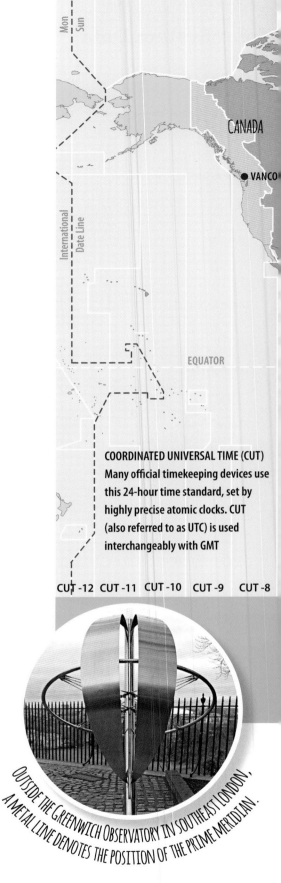

CANADA

● VANCO

International Date Line

EQUATOR

COORDINATED UNIVERSAL TIME (CUT)
Many official timekeeping devices use this 24-hour time standard, set by highly precise atomic clocks. CUT (also referred to as UTC) is used interchangeably with GMT

CUT -12 CUT -11 CUT -10 CUT -9 CUT -8

OUTSIDE THE GREENWICH OBSERVATORY IN SOUTHEAST LONDON, A METAL LINE DENOTES THE POSITION OF THE PRIME MERIDIAN.

Earth's seasons

The changing seasons on Earth are caused by its position relative to the Sun.

Summer

Fall

Spring

SUN

Winter

Why Greenwich?

When the standard for time zones was set up, Great Britain had more ships than the rest of the world put together! They were all using the **Greenwich meridian** as the prime meridian (0° longitude), so it made sense to adopt it as the international standard. And Greenwich Observatory was known for its accuracy of information, so people trusted it. Greenwich Mean Time, or GMT, became the time from which all international standard times are set.

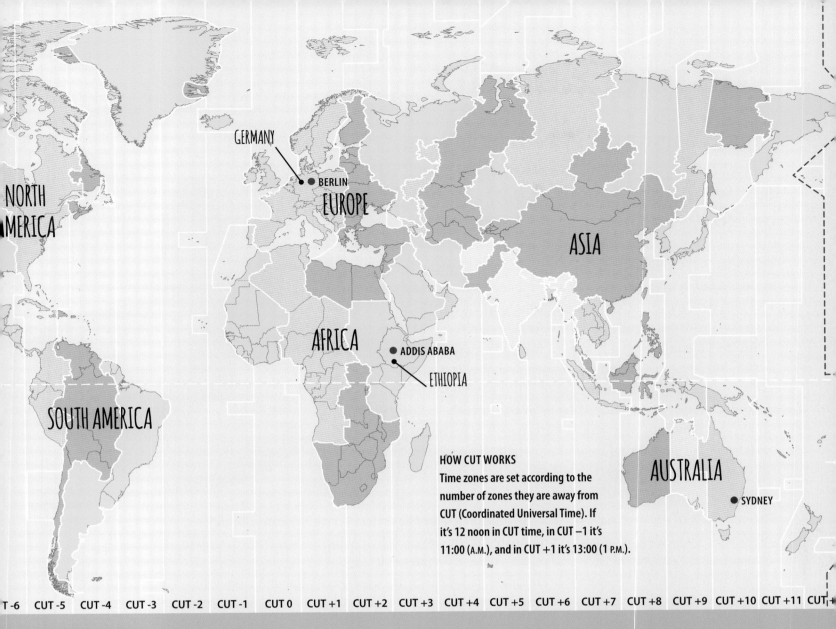

GERMANY

NORTH AMERICA

BERLIN

EUROPE

ASIA

AFRICA

ADDIS ABABA

ETHIOPIA

SOUTH AMERICA

AUSTRALIA

SYDNEY

HOW CUT WORKS
Time zones are set according to the number of zones they are away from CUT (Coordinated Universal Time). If it's 12 noon in CUT time, in CUT −1 it's 11:00 (A.M.), and in CUT +1 it's 13:00 (1 P.M.).

| T −6 | CUT −5 | CUT −4 | CUT −3 | CUT −2 | CUT −1 | CUT 0 | CUT +1 | CUT +2 | CUT +3 | CUT +4 | CUT +5 | CUT +6 | CUT +7 | CUT +8 | CUT +9 | CUT +10 | CUT +11 | CUT + |

Time Zone Map

Each time zone is based on a central meridian. These are set at 15° intervals from the prime meridian and cover the areas 7.5° to each side of the central meridian. New York City, for example, has the 75°W line of longitude as its central meridian, and its time zone includes locations between 67.5°W and 82.5°W. Time zones rarely run in straight lines north to south, however. In the U.S. they sometimes correspond with state borders, but sometimes not. In the rest of the world, time zones often follow international boundaries.

Funky French Time
Until **1911**, many French maps still showed Paris as the prime meridian, at 0°. However, legal time was said to be Paris Mean Time minus **nine minutes, 21 seconds**. This was, in fact, **GMT!**

Quiz

Zone in!
If it's 10 A.M. in Berlin, Germany, what time is it in Addis Ababa, Ethiopia?

What does "GMT" stand for?

What is the number of hours' difference between CUT −3 and CUT +3?

If you lived in Vancouver, Canada, and at 9 A.M. you called someone in Sydney, Australia, what time would it be there?

How many 15° time zones are there?

ANSWERS: 12 noon, Greenwich Mean Time, 6, 3A.M., 24

Happy New Year!
The first places to hit midnight on **December 31** are Christmas Island, Kiribati, and Samoa, so they get to celebrate **New Year's** before anyone else. Samoa used to be one of the last to see in the New Year, but it deleted a whole day, December 30, 2011, from its calendar and suddenly became the first place to see the sun set!

Inside Earth

Inside Earth there are four layers. The inner core is like a solid iron ball. It's white hot (about 9,030–12,600°F, or 5,000–7,000°C).

That's up to 70 times as hot as boiling water! However, it is under so much pressure that it can't melt, and it remains solid. The outer core is mostly iron and, although it's a little cooler than the inner core (just 7,239–9,030°F, or 4,000–5,000°C), it is liquid. This layer gives Earth its magnetic field. In addition to iron, both the outer and inner core probably contain sulfur, nickel, and small amounts of other elements. Above the outer core is the mantle, a layer of liquid rock. It flows very slowly and moves in currents as hotter rock from below rises and cools near the surface before sinking again. The crust is the part of Earth we know; the rocks, the soil, the ocean floor—and it's a very thin crust to contain all that heat!

The currents of moving rock within the mantle affect the crust. It has broken into pieces, called tectonic plates, which are constantly on the move. When they collide, they can push up mountains, and when they drift apart, huge trenches and valleys can appear. They also cause earthquakes and volcanoes. The plates that carry our continents have moved a lot since they first broke up. But you can still see some of the shapes that once fitted together.

Inner core
about 1,500 mi. (2,400 km) in diameter

Outer core
about 1,430 mi. (2,300 km) thick

Mantle
about 1,800 mi. (2,900 km) thick

Atmosphere

Crust
just 5–25 mi. (8–40 km) thick

NORTH AMERICAN PLATE

EURASIAN PLATE

CARIBBEAN PLATE

COCOS PLATE

ARABIAN PLATE

PACIFIC PLATE

PHILIPPINE PLATE

PACIFIC PLATE

AFRICAN PLATE

NAZCA PLATE

SOUTH AMERICAN PLATE

INDO-AUSTRALIAN PLATE

ANTARCTIC PLATE

Earth's riches

Fools and Their Gold

When gold is found somewhere, people flock to try to get some for themselves. Very few people find enough gold to live on, and many have sold everything they had to go searching for it. In commercial mining, a liquid metal called mercury is often used to separate the gold from the soil and other minerals around it. The mercury gets into the rivers and streams, and people and animals can be poisoned.

"This we know, the Earth does not belong to us. We belong to the Earth."

Chief Seattle

How Did Earth Form?

Like the other planets in the solar system, Earth probably formed about 4.6 billion years ago. The planets are made of molecules left over from the creation of the Sun. The molecules were floating around in a large cloud of dust, and eventually some of them bumped into each other and stuck together. Gradually these small chunks of matter collided and expanded until they formed a planet. The Sun's gravity took hold of Earth and the other planets and pulled them into its orbit, where they circle to this very day.

Precious Resources

Our planet is full of valuable resources, including precious metals, diamonds, and fossil fuels such as oil and coal. It has moving air and water, both of which can provide electricity. The oceans are full of fish, and the land teems with animals and plants that provide us with food. Yet in the process of trying to get resources from Earth, a lot can be destroyed, including people's lives and livelihoods. People are only now beginning to realize how much of an impact we humans are having on our planet, and we trying to find ways to protect it from too much damage.

Oil Spills

The oil we know about on the planet is going to run out in **less than a century**, so the oil companies are doing their best to get as much of it as they can. This includes using mining methods that harm local economies and cause oil spills both in the ocean and on land, killing numerous plants and animals.

OIL-SOAKED AFRICAN PENGUIN

Diamonds

We prize diamonds not only for their beauty but also for their usefulness in cutting: they are the hardest known natural material in the world. Yet diamonds help finance wars, too. Diamonds found in **war zones** and sold to provide money for wars or terrorism are called **"blood diamonds."** These days, diamonds that can be proved to have come from good sources have a **special certificate**.

Climate and Weather

We all know how changeable weather can be—rain one minute, bright sunshine the next; two weeks of calm followed by sudden storms.

When we talk about the weather, we usually talk about short periods of time. Climate is like a long-term view of weather. We look at what the weather does in a particular area over a long period of time, figure out the average temperatures, amount of rainfall, and other figures, and these tell us what the climate is. Tropical rain forests, for example, have a hot, damp climate. Hot, dry deserts are—well—hot and dry! But they can also get very cold at night. So plants and animals have to be able to handle the climate they live in.

Climates around the world differ for many reasons. At the equator, the central band running around Earth, the Sun shines directly overhead. This makes the climate very hot. Away from the equator, the Sun's rays are more widely spread, making the climate cooler. Mountains are generally cooler than lower land nearby. The ocean protects the land close to it from extremes of temperature, because water releases heat more slowly than land does. And climates can change over time, too. When we cut down part or all of a rain forest, the climate gets hotter. And it stays hotter for as long as it takes for the trees to grow back—if they do. This is a long-term climate change. Natural events can also change climate. El Niño, for example, is an area of unusually warm water in the Pacific Ocean that happens every two to seven years and lasts for a few months to two years. It can cause severe droughts (dry weather), floods, and crop failures in countries close to the edge of the Pacific Ocean. Fortunately, though, this is a relatively short-term climate change.

Five main climates

Climate zones
- Polar
- Cool Forest
- Temperate
- Desert
- Tropical

NORTH AMERICA

TROPIC OF CANCER

SOUTH AMERICA

TROPIC OF CAPRICORN

There are **five** main kinds of climates around the world, and they follow a rough kind of pattern. You can see this on the map above. At the extreme north and south of the globe are the freezing **polar climates**, so named because they are close to the North and South poles. At the equator are the **hot, wet tropics**. The other climate areas are in between.

Why Does Weather Happen?

The differences in temperature around the planet mean that air is constantly moving. Warm air in one place rises above cooler air, and the cooler air swirls in. In other places, cool air sinks and pushes warmer air out. Huge **"air masses,"** or bodies of air, carrying wet, dry, hot, or cold air are moved along by the wind. When two air masses meet, we get a **"front,"** and the weather changes.

Polar

At or near the poles, it's cold all the time. The ground is covered in snow and ice, and there are no crops growing. Not surprisingly, very few people live close to the poles!

Cool Forest

South of the North Pole, it's still pretty cold, but evergreen forests of pines and other conifers cover much of the land. Quite a few people live here, but they have to be prepared to dress for the cold weather!

ARCTIC CIRCLE

PRIME MERIDIAN

EUROPE

ASIA

AFRICA

EQUATOR

AUSTRALIA

Temperate

Warm summers and cool winters are typical of a temperate climate. It can be rainy all year, or the summer may be dry, but temperatures are not extreme. A lot of people choose to live in temperate regions of the world.

Tropical

Hot during the day—and not much cooler at night—tropical areas usually have rain in the afternoons. Rain forests or tropical grasslands grow here. Like those who live in the desert, the people of the rain forest have found ways of coping with the climate over many generations.

Desert

During the day, hot deserts are seriously hot! But at night they can be freezing. Most of the animals stay in their burrows in the daytime and only emerge at dusk. Most desert people have lived there for many generations. Their traditions allow them to deal with the extremes in temperature.

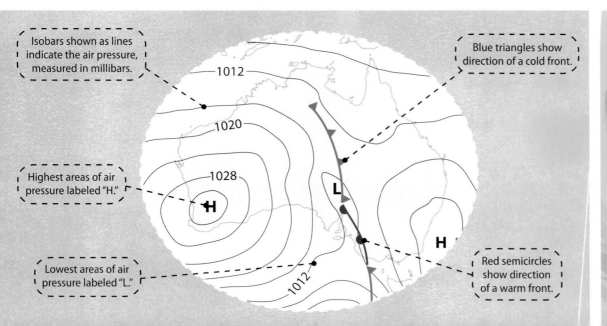

Isobars shown as lines indicate the air pressure, measured in millibars.

Blue triangles show direction of a cold front.

Highest areas of air pressure labeled "H."

Lowest areas of air pressure labeled "L."

Red semicircles show direction of a warm front.

1012

1020

1028

1012

L

H

H

Tsunami

Volcanoes and earthquakes can produce a powerful wave, called a tsunami, which grows higher as it gets close to shore. Tsunamis often appear almost without warning, and can smash buildings and uproot trees and houses over huge areas.

The World's Oceans and Seas

We think of the Sun as the most important body affecting our weather. If it's a sunny day, it'll probably be warm, and if it's cloudy, it'll be cooler.

For the most part, that's true. However, the ocean soaks up and stores heat from the Sun. In fact, the top 10 ft. (3 m) of the ocean hold the same amount of heat as the entire atmosphere does. The oceans also play a big part in whatever weather is coming our way, by flowing and drawing water and air in certain directions. The West Coast of the United States, for example, is usually mild because the winds there are warmed by the Pacific Ocean. And the oceans are also the source of most of the water in the rain cycle.

The rain cycle, also known as the water cycle, is the constant movement of water around our planet. Almost all of the water on Earth is in the oceans and seas. When the Sun heats up water in the ocean, rivers, or lakes, some of it turns into water vapor, or steam. Plants also release water vapor when they are warmed up. The vapor rises into the air until it gets cool again and forms clouds of water droplets. When there are so many water droplets that the air can't hold them anymore, we get rain (or snow or hail). This falls back into the rivers, lakes, and oceans or, if it falls on land, will run down a mountain or soak into the ground and become groundwater. Either way, it ends up back in the ocean and the whole process just keeps on going.

Freshwater

Lakes and rivers are filled with freshwater, not salty water. Although freshwater makes up only a tiny amount of the water on the surface of Earth, it still plays a large part in the **water cycle**, producing water vapor that rises and forms clouds, and then returning water that falls as rain or snow to the oceans.

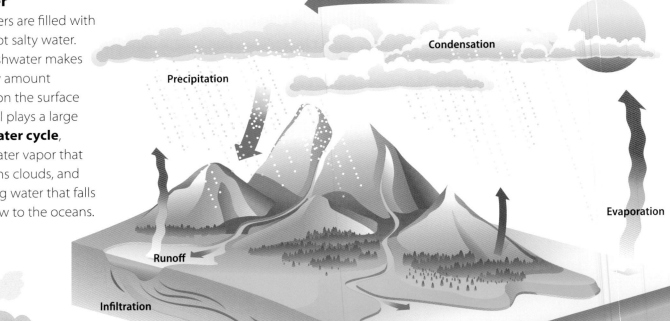

Pollution

In places where there is no good sewage system, human waste pollutes rivers and streams and can cause **disease** in people, plants, and animals. In industrialized countries, pollution from factories can contain harmful chemicals that also cause damage. It is essential for good health that the freshwater on our planet remains fresh. Many countries have laws to prevent **water pollution**.

Under the Ground

Freshwater also flows underground and is naturally filtered by the soil and stones through which it flows. People dig **wells** to reach **groundwater**, and it is often so clean that it's safe to drink. Groundwater is replenished by rain and snow and eventually flows back to the surface in **natural springs**.

Pacific Ocean

The Pacific is the largest of all the oceans. It covers about a third of Earth's surface. The Portuguese explorer Ferdinand Magellan named it the "Mar Pacifico," which means "peaceful sea" in Portuguese.

Atlantic Ocean

The Atlantic is the second-largest ocean. The world's longest mountain range is under the Atlantic. It's called the mid-Atlantic ridge, and it extends for more than 35,000 mi. (56,000 km).

Arctic Ocean

The Arctic Ocean surrounds the North Pole. It is the smallest and shallowest ocean. For much of the year the Arctic is covered in ice. When it melts, a lot of freshwater enters the ocean. Because of this, on average, it's the least salty of all the oceans.

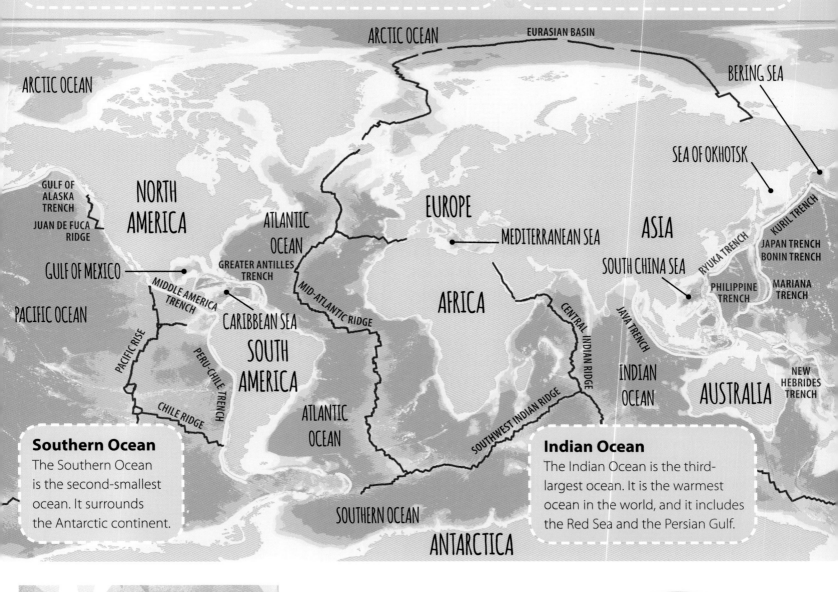

Southern Ocean

The Southern Ocean is the second-smallest ocean. It surrounds the Antarctic continent.

Indian Ocean

The Indian Ocean is the third-largest ocean. It is the warmest ocean in the world, and it includes the Red Sea and the Persian Gulf.

Why Is the Sea Salty?

Rivers and streams on land carry freshwater. But they dissolve and pick up various **minerals** from the rocks and soil that they pass through. Rivers carry the minerals with them until eventually they flow into the ocean. The **saltiness** of the oceans and seas comes from these minerals.

> "For most of history, man has had to fight nature to survive; in this century he is beginning to realize that, in order to survive, he must protect it."
>
> Jacques-Yves Cousteau

The deepest part of the ocean is Challenger Deep in the Mariana Trench, at **35,899 ft. (10,924 m)** below sea level.

The World's Population

In the 1300s the total number of people in the world was less than 400 million.

Today there are more than seven billion of us! That might sound like a success story, but the more people there are, the more pressure there is on the environment, food supplies, and other resources, such as energy. There are also more people living in poverty.

As you can see from the map on the right, people are not spread out evenly around the world. Some rich countries have a high population density, which you might expect, because they have good nutrition and health care and enough work for most people.

Part of the problem is that our resources aren't spread out evenly, either. According to experts, we produce enough food to feed everyone, but it's not always in the right place. Some people have more than they need and even waste food and water. More than 10 percent of the people in the world have too little food, and many have no access to clean water. Charities are doing their best to get food and water to those who need it, but it's a difficult job.

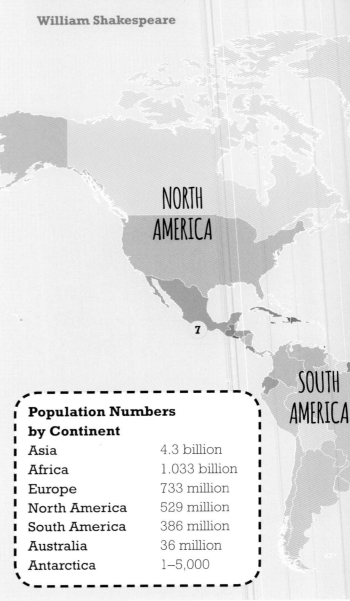

> "What is the city but the people?"
>
> William Shakespeare

NORTH AMERICA

SOUTH AMERICA

Population Numbers by Continent

Asia	4.3 billion
Africa	1.033 billion
Europe	733 million
North America	529 million
South America	386 million
Australia	36 million
Antarctica	1–5,000

Cities Are Great!

Most big cities and other large communities are close to water. Early people realized that water from rivers and streams made it possible to grow crops and to feed and water animals (and themselves!). They used boats to explore, and they met other people, with whom they could trade food and other supplies. For this they had to build more boats and ships —which created jobs. Many major cities grew up on the same spots people had first settled. People today still flock to them.

Cities Are Awful!

Cities today are becoming more and more overcrowded. They are often expensive and polluted, and yet still people arrive from outside looking for a better job and social life. Many find that life in the city is harder than they expect. They may end up with no job, no home, and no money. Even for those with good jobs, city life can be hard. Many adults move out when they have children. They believe that they can have a better family life in a less stressful environment.

Cities by Population

1. Tokyo, Japan, 35.1 million
2. Chongqing, China, 28.8 million
3. Jakarta, Indonesia, 28 million
4. Seoul, South Korea, 25.2 million
5. Delhi, India, 22.2 million
6. Manila, Phillipines, 21.9
7. Mexico City, Mexico, 21.2 million
8. Shanghai, China, 20.8 million
9. São Paulo, Brazil, 19.8 million
10. Cairo, Egypt, 19.6 million

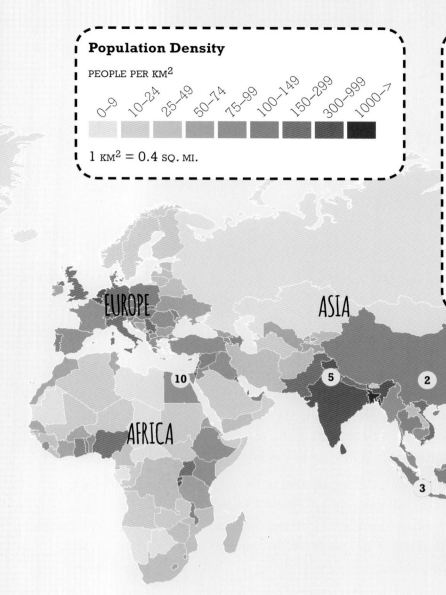

EUROPE

ASIA

AFRICA

AUSTRALIA

This map shows how early people from Africa may have spread around the world.

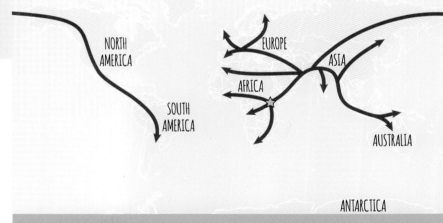

NORTH AMERICA

EUROPE

ASIA

AFRICA

SOUTH AMERICA

AUSTRALIA

ANTARCTICA

Where did we all come from?

The first hominids, or human-like mammals, developed from the ape family in Africa about five million years ago. Slowly (over millions of years) they began to walk upright and their brains grew bigger. Living and traveling in groups, they gathered fruits and other foods and hunted animals. Eventually some of our direct ancestors moved beyond Africa and humans began to dominate life all over the world.

Why do People Live in Dangerous Places?

A surprising number of people live close to **volcanoes**, in **earthquake zones**, and in areas prone to **flooding** and **forest fires**. However, close to the edges of the tectonic plates, for example, where most earthquakes and volcanoes happen, the soil is often very fertile. Precious minerals, such as gold and silver, are found there. In many cases people moved there before we knew about **plate tectonics** and realized how dangerous it was, so there were huge cities already established. And tourists wanting to see the fantastic landscapes bring in money and jobs, too!

Mapping the World

"To put a city in a book, to put the world on one sheet of paper – maps are the most condensed humanized spaces of all . . . They make the landscape fit indoors, make us masters of sights we can't see and spaces we can't cover."

Robert Harbison

Maps are drawings of places around us. We use them to help us find somewhere that we haven't been before, and they've been around a very long time.

Early maps were very inaccurate compared with those we use today, but early cartographers (mapmakers) had no detailed knowledge of the world and very often had to guess what was beyond what they knew. Gradually, better tools meant that mapmakers could improve the quality of their maps. The invention of the magnetic compass, for example, allowed more accuracy. The arrival of the printing press meant that one good map could be copied many times, making maps more affordable.

For a map to be useful, it must be relatively easy to read. Cartographers use symbols, lines, and colors to indicate different features and usually list what they all mean in a "legend," or key. Some elements of mapmaking are standard, and almost all cartographers use them. Lines of longitude and latitude, for example, make finding a place on a map easy, so you will find these on almost every map you see. However, showing a flat map of a spherical world is difficult, and there are many ways of doing it. That's why not all maps of the world are the same shape.

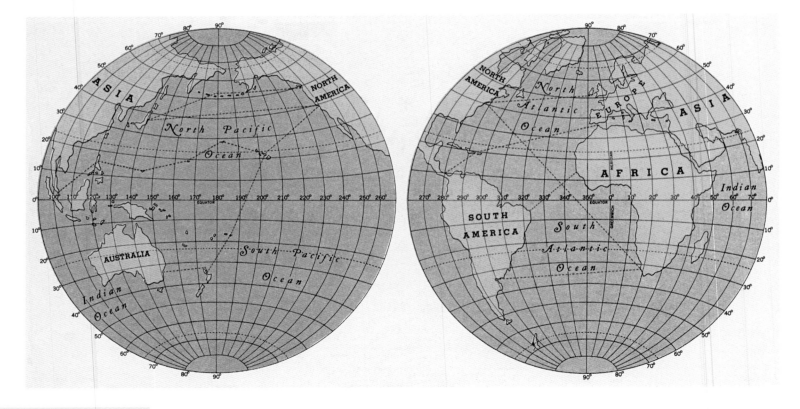

Mercator's projection

In 1659 Flemish cartographer Gerardus Mercator made a world map that presented the world as a flattened-out cylinder (tube). It became the standard "projection," or representation, of the world in two dimensions, especially for sailors, because it showed the meridians as straight lines. This made it easy to determine a course to the ship's next port of call. However, in Mercator's projection the scale (comparative size) increases toward the poles, badly distorting the shapes of some areas. Greenland, for example, looks larger than Africa, which is actually about 14 times bigger!

Robinson projection

In 1963 American cartographer Arthur H. Robinson made his world map projection an oval shape. This lessens the distortion at the poles, though it is still there. Robinson's projection is still a popular choice for maps and atlases today. However, no spherical object can be completely accurately represented in two dimensions. If you're interested in looking for different kinds of map projections, you may come across some pretty weird and wonderful alternatives.

Ocean charts

Sailors have to know not only where a place is but also how they can get there by ship—not easy when you can't see the ocean floor you're sailing over! So they have special maps called nautical charts. Depending on the scale of the chart, it may show coastlines, water depths, currents and tides, and hazards (such as rocks and shipwrecks) to avoid.

A Map for Every Occasion

*"If I had a street named after me,
it would really put me on the map."*

Jarod Kintz

Today's maps are mostly based on satellite information and are usually very accurate. The satellites orbit Earth at a low height and can record a lot of detail.

But we still need cartographers to sort through the information and turn it into readable maps that are useful in everyday life. Modern cartographers use special mapping computer software to pick out the information they need to use to create a specific kind of map.

On these pages you will see a few of the many different maps that people use in different situations. For example, to help us on short, local journeys, we use large-scale maps, which show a small area in great detail. For longer trips we use small-scale maps, which show a large area in less detail. The maps that you will see on later pages in this Atlas are small-scale.

Satellites

There are thousands of satellites orbiting Earth. Many of them have stopped working and are essentially just space junk. But many of those that still take pictures supply data that is used in making maps today.

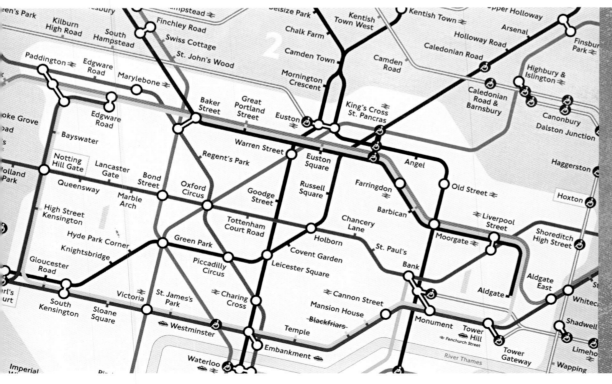

Topological Maps

A topological map is a very simple map. Maps like this usually ignore scale and detail in favor of simplicity and ease of use. Maps of subways are often topological, showing the system of lines and stations in a carefully laid-out way but disregarding their real-life distances and exact positions. Since passengers using a subway system really only want to get from one place to another, the basic information on the map is all they need.

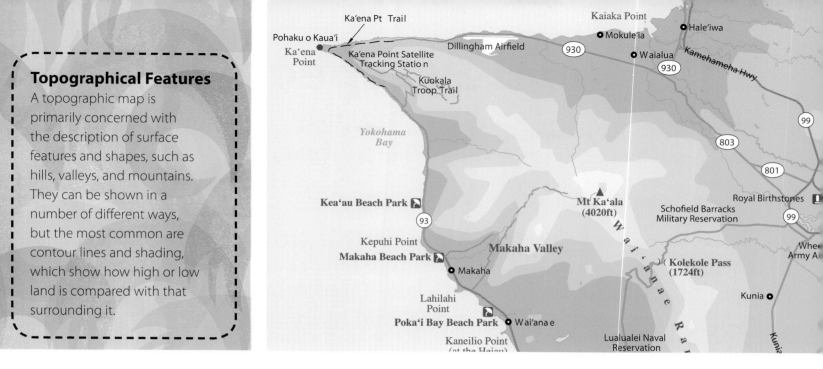

Topographical Features

A topographic map is primarily concerned with the description of surface features and shapes, such as hills, valleys, and mountains. They can be shown in a number of different ways, but the most common are contour lines and shading, which show how high or low land is compared with that surrounding it.

Street-view maps

These online maps provide a comprehensive view of a specific location. As an example, just take a look at Google's street-view maps. Their "Street View" option gives users the possibility of looking at a place almost as if they were actually there. You can zoom in, zoom out, and see buildings and other features from street level.

These maps are made using cars with nine special cameras. Together they take 360-degree images of the places they drive through. Narrow streets and other places too small for cars are mapped using tricycles— and even snowmobiles where necessary!

Flight Patterns

This map shows flight patterns of some of the world's major airlines. It demonstrates how people travel around the globe and some of the typical routes they take.

A Physical Perspective

"There isn't a parallel of latitude but thinks it would have been the equator if it had had its rights."

Mark Twain

Physical maps of the world show Earth's surface features. These usually include large ones, such as mountains, valleys, rivers, and lakes, and sometimes smaller ones, such as hills, roads, and railroad tracks.

What to include really depends on the size of the map and what it will be used for. Because they are small, the maps in this atlas show only major features. But a map meant for serious study, or to locate particular features, would be very much more detailed—and probably very much larger!

The map on the right is a physical map of part of Switzerland. On it you can see major rivers, lakes, mountains, towns and cities, and even some of the shapes of the land. You can also see country borders. These are not always included on physical maps, but they often are, because it can be useful to know in which country certain features are found.

Legend

- Rhine — River
- Lago Maggiore — Lake
- Oberalp Pass — Pass/Bridge
- Mt Titlis (3239m) — Mountain

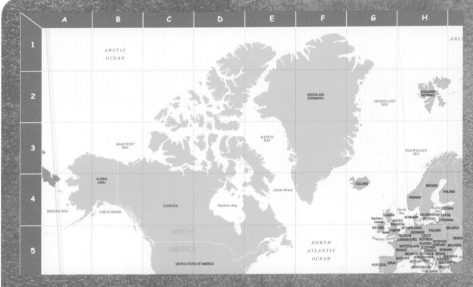

Grid references

If you want to find a specific place—say a town or city—on a map in an atlas, you will probably look it up in the index. This will give you the region or country that the town is in, the page number, and a letter and number. The letter and number form the grid reference. Find them on the edges of the map (usually the letters are at the top and the numbers down the side of the page) and trace the column down and the row inward until you find the box where they meet. Now you only have to look within that box!

Coordinates

On some maps, and especially on a globe, you might need to use coordinates to find what you are looking for. These are numbers that tell you the latitude (how far north or south somewhere is from the equator) and the longitude (how far east or west of the prime meridian). For example, the latitude and longitude of Port Elizabeth, South Africa, is 33° 55'S / 25° 34'E. This means that it's 33 degrees and 55 minutes south of the equator, and 25 degrees and 34 seconds east of the prime meridian (each degree is divided into 60 minutes). So, to find it on a map or globe, we look at the lines of latitude and longitude and find where these two coordinates meet—and there's Port Elizabeth!

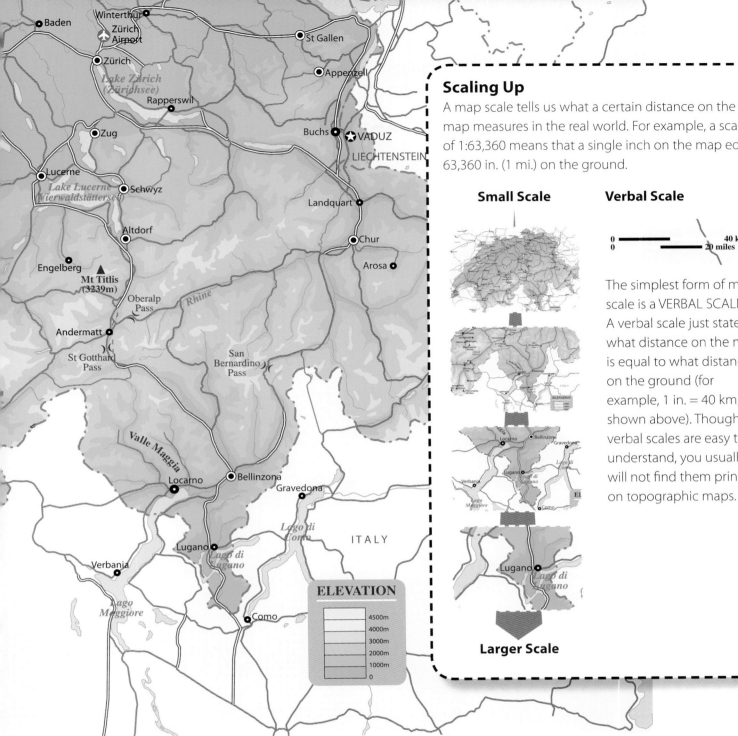

Scaling Up

A map scale tells us what a certain distance on the map measures in the real world. For example, a scale of 1:63,360 means that a single inch on the map equals 63,360 in. (1 mi.) on the ground.

Small Scale

Verbal Scale

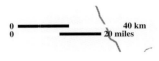

The simplest form of map scale is a VERBAL SCALE. A verbal scale just states what distance on the map is equal to what distance on the ground (for example, 1 in. = 40 km, as shown above). Though verbal scales are easy to understand, you usually will not find them printed on topographic maps.

Larger Scale

ELEVATION

4500m
4000m
3000m
2000m
1000m
0

How to read a hiker's map

Many of us don't need to know how to find our way across landscapes on foot. Cars, airplanes, and other kinds of transportation usually take us over long distances. But if we want to go exploring out in the country, we need a map with good detail and landmarks that we can use to be sure we're going the right way! Large-scale maps, such as this hiker's map, show enough detail to allow you to be sure you're going in the right direction.

A Political Perspective

"You have brains in your head. You have feet in your shoes. You can steer yourself any direction you choose."

Dr. Seuss

Political maps in a detailed atlas, like the one below, include specific kinds of information.

They are intended to show the countries of the world and the land that each controls. National and state borders are clearly marked, and not only capital cities but also other cities and large towns are marked with a symbol and labeled. Often, countries are colored differently from those next to them to make it clear where each one begins and ends. There are special kinds of lines for borders that are in dispute—for example, where two countries are arguing or fighting over an area of land. Really large physical features, such as mountain ranges and major rivers, are sometimes shown, but not always.

Things change a lot in the political world! After World War II, for example, Germany was split into two—East Germany and West Germany. Maps had to be redrawn to show this. Then, in 1990, they were reunited, and the maps were redrawn again. Sometimes places change their names to reflect new political leadership. The old name as well as the new one may be shown for a while to help people who don't know about the change. Issues like this mean that political maps usually become out of date much more quickly than physical maps.

As you will have noticed, most countries don't come in nice, neat shapes. Where a country controls somewhere far away from its homeland, such as Alaska in the United States, cartographers often use a separate inset box to highlight that it doesn't physically belong in the part of the world shown on the map.

	International boundary
	Traditional boundary of the princely state of Jammu and Kashmir
	Line of Control
	Internal administrative boundary
	Indian State of Jammu and Kashmir
	Pakistani-controlled areas of Kashmir

0   50   100 Kilometres

Border fighting
Sometimes more than one country lays claim to a region or territory. Southern Asia's Kashmir, for example, has been at the center of a dispute between India and Pakistan for more than 60 years! There is no international recognition of either claim to the area, so Kashmir is shown as a disputed territory on maps like this. Disputed territories have dotted borders on the maps in this book.

North America

"America is so vast that almost everything said about it is likely to be true, and the opposite is probably equally true."

James T. Farrell

MAP KEY
1 Vaquita **2** Golden Gate Bridge **3** Giant redwood **4** Canadian goose **5** Moose **6** Puffin **7** Mount Rushmore **8** **The** Capitol **9** Statue of Liberty **10** Midwestern farm **11** Mississippi steamboat **12** Alligator **13** Mexico City Metropolitan Cathedral **14** Mayan temple, Tikal **15** Ackee

ALASKA

YUKON TERRITORY

GULF OF ALASKA

BRITISH COLUMBIA

WASHINGTON

OREGON

NORTH PACIFIC OCEAN

HAWAII

Area: 9.5 million sq. mi. (24.5 million km²)
Fact: third-largest continent (after Asia and Africa)
Population: 529 million

North America has 22 named time zones, but many of them are the same. In fact, there are really only five different time zones on the continent.

North America is packed full of natural wonders. From Niagara Falls to Death Valley, from the Grand Canyon to Mount McKinley, it has some of the most amazing landscapes in the world.

It is the third-largest continent and has all of the major climate types. This gives it a truly diverse range of plants and animals, including one of the smallest owls and the largest bears. The continent is also home to a multitude of people from all over the world and contains some of the largest cities.

The first North American people were from Asia. They developed a number of different cultures and languages. Most of them hunted animals and gathered fruit, nuts, and vegetables for food. In the south, some learned how to cultivate crops, such as corn and tomatoes. The Maya people, in Central America, developed a system of writing and an advanced calendar. When European people arrived in the 1500s, not only did they bring a rich cultural heritage but also diseases, such as smallpox and flu, that wiped out huge numbers of Native Americans.

ARCTIC OCEAN

GREENLAND

BAFFIN BAY

NORTHWEST TERRITORIES

NUNAVUT

HUDSON BAY

QUEBEC

NEWFOUNDLAND & LABRADOR

PRINCE EDWARD ISLAND

ALBERTA

SASKATCHEWAN

MANITOBA

ONTARIO

MONTANA

N. DAKOTA

MINNESOTA

WISCONSIN

NEW YORK

MAINE

NEW BRUNSWICK

NOVA SCOTIA

IDAHO

WYOMING

Mississippi R.

NEW HAMPSHIRE
MASSACHUSETTS
CONNECTICUT
NEW JERSEY
DELAWARE

NEVADA

NEBRASKA

IOWA

Missouri R.

ILLINOIS

INDIANA

OHIO

PENNSYLVANIA

UTAH

COLORADO

KANSAS

MISSOURI

Ohio R.

KENTUCKY

W. VIRGINIA

VIRGINIA

ARIZONA

CALIFORNIA

NEW MEXICO

OKLAHOMA

TENNESSEE

NORTH CAROLINA

BERMUDA

TEXAS

SOUTH CAROLINA

GEORGIA

FLORIDA

NORTH ATLANTIC OCEAN

MEXICO

LOUISIANA

GULF OF MEXICO

BAHAMAS

CUBA

DOMINICAN REPUBLIC

CARIBBEAN

BELIZE

PUERTO RICO

HONDURAS

GUATEMALA

NICARAGUA

CARIBBEAN SEA

EL SALVADOR

COSTA RICA

PANAMA

SOUTH AMERICA

North America—Big and Beautiful!

Sometimes it seems that North America does everything in a big way! It's known for big buildings, huge lakes, enormous waterfalls, and other physical features. North American people even think big; just look at the number of new ideas that have come from here. From walking on the Moon to inventing the nuclear bomb to creating jazz, country, and mariachi music, and building enormous theme parks. Not to mention Hollywood's booming movie industry, which makes countless North Americans and others from around the world into huge, box-office-busting, moneymaking stars!

North America grows about half of the world's corn

BOURBON STREET IN THE FRENCH QUARTER, NEW ORLEANS

MORAINE LAKE IN THE CANADIAN ROCKY MOUNTAINS

GOLDEN GATE BRIDGE, SAN FRANCISCO

THE GRAND CANYON, ARIZONA

Why "America"?

America was named after the 15th-century Italian explorer Amerigo Vespucci. He was the first person to think that the South American continent was not part of the East Indies but a different land, previously unknown to Europeans. The name "America" was later extended to North America.

NORTH AMERICA TOP 10

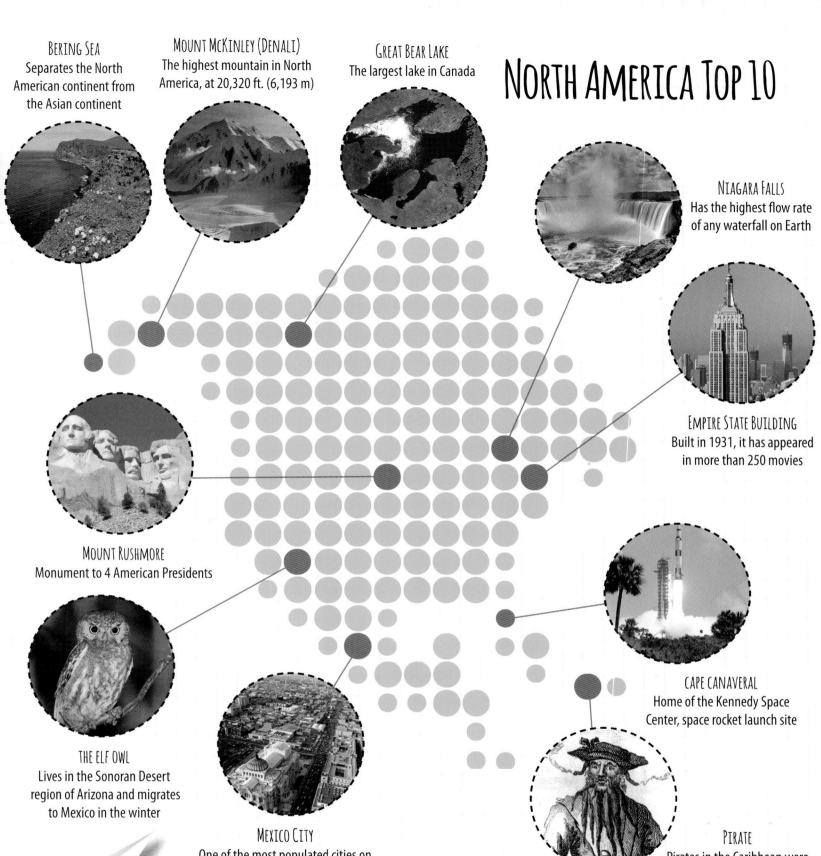

BERING SEA
Separates the North American continent from the Asian continent

MOUNT MCKINLEY (DENALI)
The highest mountain in North America, at 20,320 ft. (6,193 m)

GREAT BEAR LAKE
The largest lake in Canada

NIAGARA FALLS
Has the highest flow rate of any waterfall on Earth

EMPIRE STATE BUILDING
Built in 1931, it has appeared in more than 250 movies

MOUNT RUSHMORE
Monument to 4 American Presidents

THE ELF OWL
Lives in the Sonoran Desert region of Arizona and migrates to Mexico in the winter

MEXICO CITY
One of the most populated cities on Earth, with nine million inhabitants

CAPE CANAVERAL
Home of the Kennedy Space Center, space rocket launch site

PIRATE
Pirates in the Caribbean were also known as buccaneers

ALL-AMERICAN HEROES

Many North Americans are famous all over the world—for example, **Neil Armstrong** (left), the first man to walk on the Moon. **Sitting Bull** was a Sioux medicine man and holy man who defeated **General Custer** at the battle of Little Bighorn. Famous North American writers include **Mark Twain** (right) and **Maya Angelou**. Musicians such as **Dizzy Gillespie** and **Avril Lavigne** have made a splash, as have actors **Will Smith** and **Jennifer Lawrence**.

CANADA

Alberta - British Columbia - Manitoba - New Brunswick
Newfoundland & Labrador - Nova Scotia - Ontario
Prince Edward Island - Quebec - Saskatchewan

Canada is a vast, rugged land. From north to south it
spans more than half of the Northern Hemisphere. From
east to west it stretches almost 4,700 mi. (7,560 km).
Winters can be very cold, with temperatures dropping
below −40°F (−40°C) in some parts of the country.
However, the huge forest that covers much of Canada's
land is home to millions of different birds and other
wildlife. Canada is famous for its large mammals, which
include bears, caribou (wild reindeer), gray wolves,
moose, mountain lions, musk oxen, walrus, and whales.

MOOSE ALERT!
Moose warning signs are used on roads in regions
where there is a danger of cars colliding with moose.

INUIT FAMILY IN IGLOO, NUNAVUT, CANADA

YUKON
TERRITORY

Great Bear Lake

WHITEHORSE

NORTHWEST
TERRITORIES

ALBERTA

EDMONTON

BRITISH
COLUMBIA

GULF OF
ALASKA

VICTORIA

A BULL MOOSE CAN
HAVE ANTLERS UP TO
6 FT. (1.8 M) ACROSS

NEXT
5 km

ARCTIC
OCEAN

GREENLAND

BAFFIN
BAY

NUNAVUT

ELLOWKNIFE

Great Slave Lake

HUDSON
BAY

NORTH
ATLANTIC
OCEAN

ASKATCHEWAN

MANITOBA

Lake
Winnipeg

NEWFOUNDLAND
& LABRADOR

REGINA

Lake
Manitoba

ONTARIO

QUEBEC

WINNIPEG

PRINCE EDWARD ISLAND

QUEBEC CITY

ST. JOHN'S

Lake Superior

MONTREAL

NEW
BRUNSWICK

OTTAWA

Lake Huron

TORONTO

FREDERICTON

HALIFAX

Lake Ontario

NOVA SCOTIA

Lake Erie

THE FAST AND THE FURRY

The fastest land animal in Canada is the pronghorn, which looks a little like an antelope. It can reach almost **55 mph (90 km/h)** over short distances.
The Atlantic puffin is the smallest puffin in the world, about the size of a pigeon. It has to flap its wings about **300 to 400 times** a minute to fly!
The arctic fox has the warmest pelt (fur) of all arctic animals and is the smallest of all canids (dogs, wolves, and foxes) in the Arctic.

AT HOME IN THE ROCKIES

The Canadian Rocky Mountains are part of a series of mountain ranges running from Alaska to the tip of South America. They are home to hundreds of elks, bighorn sheep, and moose, as well as many other animals.

BIGHORN SHEEP

?

WHO OR WHAT AM I?

I hatch in a nest on the ground, in the mountains of Alaska and Canada. I'm white in the winter, but my back gets brown in the summer. My name begins with a silent letter.

ANSWER: A ptarmigan

WHO LIVES HERE?

The original inhabitants of Canada were the **Native Americans**, or First Nations people. **Europeans** settled the country in the 1600s, and their descendants also live here, along with more recent immigrants. Most **Canadians** speak English, but French is also an official language.

The name **Canada** comes from the word "kanata" which means "settlement" or "village" in the language of the indigenous St. Lawrence Iroquoians.

MAD ABOUT MAPLE

Since 1965, the maple leaf has been the centerpiece of the national flag of Canada. Maple tree sap is used to make delicious maple syrup. It takes 30–50 gal. (115–190 L) of sap to make just 1 gal. (4 L) of syrup. In the fall, maple leaves change color to vibrant oranges, reds, and russets, and the national parks publish color reports so that tourists can find the best places to spot this glorious sight.

5,526 mi. (8,893 km) of border is shared between the **U.S. and Canada.** It's the largest shared border in the world

For 94 years the **Jasper Raven Totem Pole** stood in Jasper National Park. But when it was found to be rotten, it was sent back to the Haida Nation that had carved it. In 2011 the Two Brothers Totem Pole was sent to replace the original.

Canadians use a number of slang terms for their **money.** The $1 coin, for example, has a picture of a common loon (a kind of bird) on it, so it's often called a **"loonie."** The $2 coin is called a **"toonie,"** a combination of the words "two" and "loonie"!

Canada has between **two and three million lakes** —that's more than all the other countries in the world put together!

20% of all water on Earth is contained in Canada's lakes.

JOB:
Forestry

ART:
Inuit carvings in walrus ivory, muskox horn, caribou antler, and soapstone; totem poles

WHAT TO SAY:
"Take off!" (You're kidding, no way)

WHAT NOT TO SAY:
Are you American?

FOOD:
Poutine—french fries, topped with a light brown gravy-like sauce and cheese curds

LEISURE ACTIVITY:
Trips to watch polar bears

SWEET TREAT:
Maple syrup

The game of **lacrosse** that so many Canadians play today is based on traditional games played by a number of different **First Nations** communities. This makes it one of the oldest team sports in North America! Traditionally, some games could last for days, and up to 1,000 people from local villages took part.

NORTHWEST TERRITORIES
T6169
CANADA N.W.T. 83 1983

License plates for cars, motorcycles, and snowmobiles in the Northwest Territories are in the shape of a **polar bear.**

Canada is rich in minerals, including zinc, nickel, lead, and gold. Since the 1500s, it has exported fish and furs around the world.

Canadians eat more macaroni and cheese than any other people in the world!

FALL LEAVES CHANGING COLOR

NORTH PACIFIC OCEAN

ALLIGATORS IN AMERICA CAN GROW UP TO 11 FT. (3.4 M).

EASTERN UNITED STATES

ALABAMA - CONNECTICUT - DELAWARE - FLORIDA - GEORGIA - ILLINOIS - INDIANA
KENTUCKY - MAINE - MARYLAND - MASSACHUSETTS - MICHIGAN - MISSISSIPPI - NEW HAMPSHIRE -
NEW JERSEY - NEW YORK - NORTH CAROLINA - OHIO - PENNSYLVANIA - RHODE ISLAND -
SOUTH CAROLINA - TENNESSEE - VERMONT - VIRGINIA - WEST VIRGINIA - WISCONSIN

The eastern United States is a vastly diverse region. In the north are bustling metropolises like New York City, Chicago and Philadelphia that bristle with skyscrapers. The south of the region is hotter and is known for a more relaxed pace of life. Many famous pop, country and blues stars come from this region, from states like Tennessee, Mississippi and Georgia. Even further south, people flock to Florida for its sunshine, beaches and world-famous theme parks.

THE FIRST, THE FARTHEST, AND THE TOOTHIEST . . .

One World Trade Center, in New York City, is a shiny steel structure, and the spire climbs up to **1,176 ft. (541 m)**. It is a replacement for the old World Trade Center, which was destroyed in a terrorist attack in 2001 ● America's first undersea national park, John Pennekamp Coral Reef State Park, was created in 1960. It has an underwater statue of Jesus Christ, a submerged Spanish ship, and lots of incredible, protected coral! ● The farthest south you can go in the continental U.S.A is the end of Key West, Florida. It's marked by a giant concrete buoy and features in many tourist photos ● Only one kind of crocodile and one kind of alligator live in the U.S., and both of them are found in the mangrove swamps of the Florida Everglades.

STATE OF THE NATION

The United States is a relatively young country. Its first people, the Native Americans, didn't see themselves as part of a larger nation. When European settlers arrived, they began to take over the land, fighting the Native Americans for control. In 1783, 13 colonies on the East Coast, previously under British rule, won their independence and the United States was born.

Lake Superior

Lake Huron

WISCONSIN

Lake Michigan

MICHIGAN

Lake Erie

NEW HAMPSHIRE
VERMONT

MASSACHUSETTS

MAINE

NEW YORK

CHICAGO

ILLINOIS

INDIANA

OHIO

PENNSYLVANIA

BOSTON

RHODE ISLAND

NEW YORK CITY

CONNECTICUT
NEW JERSEY

Mississippi R.

Ohio R.

KENTUCKY

W. VIRGINIA

VIRGINIA

DELAWARE

MARYLAND

WASHINGTON, D.C.

NORTH
ATLANTIC
OCEAN

35
million Americans share **DNA** with at least one of the 102 pilgrims who arrived aboard the **Mayflower** in 1620.

TENNESSEE

N. CAROLINA

MISSISSIPPI

SOUTH
CAROLINA

ALABAMA

GEORGIA

FLORIDA

TAMPA

MIAMI

THE STATUE OF LIBERTY

U.S. POSTAGE 11¢

IN GOD WE TRUST

LIBERTY

The seven rays on the crown of the **Statue of Liberty** represent the seven continents. Each measures up to **9 ft. (2.7 m)** in length and weighs as much as **150 lb. (70 kg)**.

WHO LIVES HERE?

The United States' population is made up of people from all over the world. As well as **Native American** families and the descendants of the European settlers, there are **African Americans**, many of whom are descended from freed slaves. And people flock to the United States today, seeing it as a land of opportunity, and wanting their chance at the "American Dream."

In 1620, **settlers from the UK** arrived in what is now Massachusetts. Their first winter was very difficult, with little food to eat. But some **Native Americans** taught them how to farm local crops, and in their second year they had a good harvest. They invited the Native Americans who had helped them to join them for a meal. That meal is still celebrated today, as **Thanksgiving Day.**

GRUB'S UP

American food has been influenced by cuisines from all over the world. However, there are some dishes that Americans really can call their own— and they're delicious! Corn dogs were invented in Texas; Ruth Graves Wakefield of Massachusetts came up with the chocolate-chip cookie.

Most of the world's tornadoes occur in the Midwest region of the U.S., known as **Tornado Alley**

The most populous **city** in the United States is **New York City**, followed by Los Angeles and Chicago.

THE EASTERN U.S. REAL DEAL!

WHAT TO SAY:
Have a nice day!

WHAT NOT TO SAY:
Football is stupid!

FAMOUS FOR:
Key lime pie

SPORTS:
Football, surfing, inline skating

DRINKS:
Ginger ale, iced tea

FOOD:
Hot dogs, clam chowder, fried green tomatoes, crawfish

George Washington Carver, who lived in Alabama, discovered more than **300** uses for **peanuts.** Carver wanted to help poor farmers by finding alternative crops to cotton, such as peanuts and sweet potatoes, which would also help feed the farmers' families.

6% of people in the **U.S.** believe nobody has ever landed on the **Moon.**

In 2014 the US became the biggest producer of oil in the world, overtaking Saudi Arabia and Russia. Much of the oil comes from offshore drilling in the Gulf of Mexico.

The American **one-dollar bill** contains several hidden images, including a spider in the upper-right-hand corner.

ALASKA

HAWAII

WESTERN UNITED STATES

ALASKA - ARIZONA - ARKANSAS - CALIFORNIA - COLORADO - HAWAII - IDAHO - IOWA - KANSAS - LOUSIANA - MINNESOTA - MISSOURI - MONTANA - NEBRASKA - NEVADA - NEW MEXICO - NORTH DAKOTA - SOUTH DAKOTA - OKLAHOMA - OREGON - TEXAS - UTAH - WASHINGTON - WYOMING

In the western states are many of the incredible landscapes that the United States is famous for. Much of the middle of the country is covered in prairies – grasslands that are perfect for farming. Further west are the towering snowy peaks of the Rocky Mountains, as well as one of the hottest places on earth – a sweltering desert called Death Valley, in the state of California. West of the deserts and mountains lie the high-tech cities of the West Coast – where new phones and computers are invented and movies are made.

DUSTY DESERTS
Most of Arizona is made up of deserts.

TEXAS LONGHORN

THE AURORA BOREALIS (NORTHERN LIGHTS) IS AN AMAZING SPECTACLE

California is where the high-tech Silicon Valley is located.

SILICON VALLEY

SEATTLE

WASHINGTON

PORTLAND

OREGON

IDAHO

MONTANA

NORTH DAKOTA

MINNESOTA

Lake Superior

SOUTH DAKOTA

WYOMING

NEBRASKA

Missouri R.

IOWA

Mississippi R.

MISSOURI

NEVADA

DENVER

SACRAMENTO

SAN FRANCISCO

LAS VEGAS

UTAH

COLORADO

KANSAS

WICHITA

ST. LOUIS

CALIFORNIA

LOS ANGELES

ARIZONA

ALBUQUERQUE

PHOENIX

NEW MEXICO

OKLAHOMA

ARKANSAS

DALLAS

TEXAS

HOUSTON

LOUISIANA

NEW ORLEANS

MODERN PUEBLOS IN NEW MEXICO ARE BASED ON THE ANCIENT ARCHITECTURE OF NATIVE AMERICANS

NORTH PACIFIC OCEAN

GULF OF MEXICO

WHO LIVES HERE?

In the Southwest of the United States it is common to find inhabitants with Mexican ancestry. There's also a strong mix of Hispanic people from Central and South America, as well as descendants of European settlers and African Americans.

Almost **40 million people** live in California—one-eighth of the entire U.S.

Surfing began in Hawaii. (It was noted by **Captain Cook** in 1778.) Now the sport is practiced all over the world.

Hawaii is the most recent of the 50 states in the U.S. (it joined in **1959**).

SURF'S UP!

ALOHA, HAWAII

Many people dream of living in a place like Hawaii. It's certainly beautiful, warm, and sunny, and it is the center of the surfing world, with some of the tallest and cleanest waves around. Oahu's North Shore has many surfing destinations that play host to thousands of amateurs, pros, and wannabe pros from around the world each year.

The **U.S.** bought Alaska from **Russia** in 1867 for **$7.2 million.** It's the largest state in the country.

WHAT TO SAY:
"Howdy!"

FAMOUS FOR:
Cowboys

INFAMOUS FOR:
Hollywood

POPULAR FOOD:
Peanut butter and jelly sandwiches

HOBBY:
Storm chasing

PLANT:
Saguaro cactus

In **California** you can go from **282 ft.** (86 m) below sea level in Death Valley to **14,494 ft.** (4,418 m) above at the top of Mt. Whitney in less than a day.

U.S. Highway 550 in Colorado became known as Million Dollar Highway because its roadbed was paved with low-grade gold ore.

US 550

5,064 years old (in 2014), a **bristlecone pine** in California's White Mountains is the **oldest** known **living tree** in the world

500,000 or so measurable seismic tremors happen in California each year.

Silicon Valley in California is home to many of the world's most famous companies including Apple, who make phones and tablets, and Pixar, who make animated movies.

The tallest mountain in Hawaii is **Mauna Kea**. It's **13,796 ft.** (4,205 m) above sea level.

98% of the world's crawfish are caught in the state of Lousiana.

However, when measured from the sea floor, it is more than **32,000 ft.** (10,000 m) high, making it taller than Mount Everest (Earth's highest mountain above sea level, at **29,028 ft.** (8,848 m).

MEXICO, CENTRAL AMERICA, AND THE CARIBBEAN

Belize - Caribbean Islands - Costa Rica - El Salvador - Guatemala - Honduras - Mexico - Nicaragua - Panama

Mexico is a land of extremes, with high mountains and deep canyons in the center of the country, sweeping deserts in the north, and dense rain forests in the south and east. Southeast of Mexico is Central America, a narrow strip of land that connects North America to South America. Overall, the land is fertile and rugged and is dominated by a series of volcanic mountain ranges.

Central America is bordered by Colombia, the Caribbean Sea, and the Pacific Ocean. Directly to the east are the islands of the Caribbean. The rain forests and coastal wetlands of eastern Mexico are home to thousands of tropical plant species and exotic animals such as jaguars and quetzal birds. Few countries on Earth support as many plant and animal species as Mexico does. Rain forests are also common in Central America, especially Panama and Costa Rica.

GREAT VIEW!
The church of Nuestra Señora de los Remedios in Mexico was built on top of the ruins of the ancient pyramid Tlachihualtepetl. It looks out toward the active volcano Popocatépetl.

MEXICO

NORTH PACIFIC OCEAN

FRENCH PIRATE FRANÇOIS L'OLONNAIS OPERATED IN THE CARIBBEAN IN THE 1660S

BAHAMAS

GULF OF MEXICO

QUETZAL BIRD

CUBA

HAVANA

DOMINICAN REPUBLIC

MEXICO CITY

BELIZE CITY

SANTO DOMINGO

CARIBBEAN SEA

JAMAICA

HAITI

CARIBBEAN

GUATEMALA CITY

BELIZE

GUATEMALA

PUERTO RICO

HONDURAS

EL SALVADOR

TEGUCIGALPA

A LIONFISH, AN INVASIVE SPECIES, ON A CORAL REEF

SAN SALVADOR

NICARAGUA

Lake Managua

TEOTIHUACAN MASK
MEXICO

MANAGUA

Lake Nicaragua

COSTA RICA

PANAMA CITY

SAN JOSÉ

PANAMA

PEAKS AND REEFS

The highest mountain in Mexico is Pico de Orizaba, a dormant volcano that reaches **18,491 ft. (5,636 m)** above sea level • The vaquita is the smallest of all the cetaceans (porpoises, whales, and dolphins), growing up to about **55 in. (140 cm)**. It is also the most endangered and is only found off the coast of Mexico, at the northern end of the Gulf of California • The Mesoamerican Barrier Reef System stretches from Cancún to Honduras. At about **560 mi. (900 km)** long, it is one of the largest coral reef systems in the world. The Belize Barrier Reef, which is part of it, is Belize's top tourist destination and brings in almost half of the country's **260,000** or more annual visitors.

PANAMA CANAL

The Panama Canal allows ships to cross Central America between the Pacific and Atlantic oceans, saving them the longer and more dangerous journey around South America. The canal crosses 51 mi. (82 km) of Panama. It was begun in 1881 and completed in 1914 and is known as one of the seven modern wonders of the world.

32 USA

EL CASTILLO, CHICHEN ITZA, ALSO KNOWN AS THE TEMPLE OF KUKULKAN

WHO LIVES HERE?

Native Americans were the region's first real occupants. From the 1500s onward the majority of the area was colonized by **Spain**. Most of today's Central Americans and Caribbean people are of mixed heritage, and the population includes **African, Asian, European, and Native American people.**

The Spanish invaded **Yucatan** in the 1500s. It's said they gave it its name because whenever they asked a question, the indigenous Mayas replied **"Uh yu ka t'ann,"** which meant **"Hear how they talk"**!

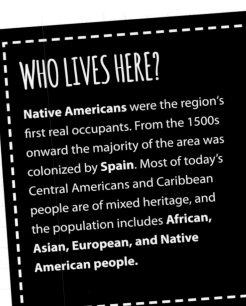

CRAZY ABOUT SOCCER

Mexicans adore soccer—it's their most popular sport, and they're pretty good at it, with the national team reaching the World Cup quarterfinals twice. The fans at the national stadium, Estadio Azteca in Mexico City, are famous for doing the "wave." This is when fans stand up one after another and raise their arms above their head, creating a ripple effect in the crowd. The wave caught on worldwide after it was done at the 1986 World Cup, held in Mexico.

The islands of the **Caribbean** trade in fish, aluminum, iron, nickel, petroleum, and timber

La Catrina is an icon of Mexican pop art. She is often seen on display during **Día de los Muertos (Day of the Dead)** celebrations in Mexico.

97% of **Barbadians** can read and write. The island nation's educational system is not only very good, but also free to all children.

117 million people live in **Mexico**. It is the 11th most populated country in the world.

MUSIC:
Mexican mariachi bands

FOOD:
Mole is a Mexican savory sauce

PLACE:
Trafalgar Falls, Dominica

FESTIVAL:
Día de Los Muertos (Day of the Dead)

SAYING (JAMAICAN) :
Wan han wash de oda (One hand washes the other)

GAME:
Lotería is a popular game, similar to bingo but with singing and picture cards

SPORT:
Soccer is the most popular sport in Mexico, but other favorites include baseball and jai alai, a handball game that began in Spain

FRUIT:
Ackee is a yellow fruit that must be eaten ripe —it's poisonous otherwise!

Mexicans take sports seriously. In ancient times, losers of a ritual ball game were **put to death**. In some dangerous sports, such as bullfighting and **rodeo** (which was invented in Mexico), competitors still put their lives on the line.

42 million people live in Central America.

Mexico produces oil, silver, copper, and agricultural products. Central America mines copper, gold, silver, and zinc.

There are many **volcanoes** in Central America (it's on the **Ring of Fire**), including 28 active ones.

Saint Lucia changed hands between the French and British **14 times** in the 1600s and 1700s.

GALÁPAGOS ISLANDS
(ECUADOR)

EQUATOR

SOUTH
PACIFIC OCEAN

South America

"The forest is not a resource for us, it is life itself. It is the only place for us to live."

Evaristo Nugkuag Ikanan, Peruvian campaigner (born 1950) and activist for the Aguaruna people of the Peruvian rain forest

South America is a land of legends. Hundreds of years ago, explorers from Europe heard rumors of lost kingdoms and cities, of fabulous treasure, and of peoples living deep in the forests. The truth was more wonderful than the tales. South America had ancient civilizations, great empires—such as that of the Incas—skilled goldsmiths, builders, and craftspeople— and chocolate!

Spanish and Portuguese invaders arrived in the 1500s. They had guns, ships, and horses and were greedy for land and gold. They ruled for almost 300 years.

But today's independent South American nations are home to a rich mixture of peoples, beliefs, and cultures. Their roots are indigenous, European, African, and Asian. Yet amid the farms, the factories, the slums, and the skyscrapers, the ancient spirit of South America survives in a love of ritual and spectacle, of music and color, of people working together. The mountains and ancient forests are still there, too, but in many places they are under threat from loggers and miners. For the future of South America and the rest of the world, they too must survive.

10

South America has five time zones, if you count the remote Pacific islands of the Galápagos, which belong to Ecuador. As the largest country, Brazil straddles several zones.

MAP KEY
1 Ocelot 2 Red cayenne peppers 3 Green turtle
4 Machu Picchu 5 Scarlet macaw 6 Sawn logs
7 Totora reed canoe, Lake Titicaca 8 Coffee
beans 9 Christ the Redeemer, Rio de Janeiro
10 South American sea lion 11 Iguaçú Falls

Area: 6,890,000 sq. mi. (17,840,000 km²)
Fact: fourth-largest continent
Population: 389,860,000

SOUTH AMERICA
IS HERE!

LPELO ISLAND
(COLOMBIA)

Orinoco R.

VENEZUELA

GUYANA

SURINAME

1

COLOMBIA

ECUADOR

PERU

Andes

BOLIVIA

Lake Titicaca

Amazon River basin

FRENCH GUIANA

Amazon R.

BRAZIL

2

3

EQUATOR

5

4

Brazilian
Highlands

6

7

Atacama
Desert

PARAGUAY

8

9

CHILE

Gran Chaco

Mar Chiquita

11

Andes

URUGUAY

ARGENTINA

Pampas

SOUTH
ATLANTIC
OCEAN

Patagonia

FALKLAND ISLANDS
(U.K.)

SOUTH GEORGIA
(U.K.)

TIERRA
DEL FUEGO

CAPE HORN

Incredible South America

The Amazon River rises in Peru, in the Andes Mountains. It flows eastward across Brazil to the Atlantic Ocean. Smallmotor boats beat against the current, passing remote fishing and trading villages. The Amazon basin forms the green heart of South America and is covered by the world's largest rain forest. To the north, the Guiana highlands drop to tropical plains beside the Caribbean Sea and the Atlantic. Eastward, the dizzying peaks of the Andes form a long, rocky backbone, parallel to the Pacific coast. Along the Atlantic coast are huge cities. As the landmass narrows in the south, there are coffee plantations, hot and dusty scrub, cattle ranches, and grasslands. In the far south, bleak valleys stretch toward frozen Antarctica.

The **Andes mountain** chain is the world's longest, at approx. **4,300 mi.** (7,000 km)

Lake Titicaca, Bolivia

Tierra del Fuego

Erupting Volcano, Chile

Galápagos Islands (Ecuador)

Amazon Rain Forest

Awesome Amazon

The Amazon rain forest covers approximately **2.1 million sq. mi. (5.5 million km²)** ● It takes in **nine** countries ● It receives a massive **108 in. (2,743 mm)** of rainfall a year ● The trees produce about **one-fifth** of all our planet's life-giving oxygen ● The forest supports a greater **variety** of species than anywhere else on Earth ● **10%** of the world's known species and **20%** of the world's bird species live here ● There are **500** mammal species, an estimated **2.5 million** different **insects**, and **40,000** different **plants**.

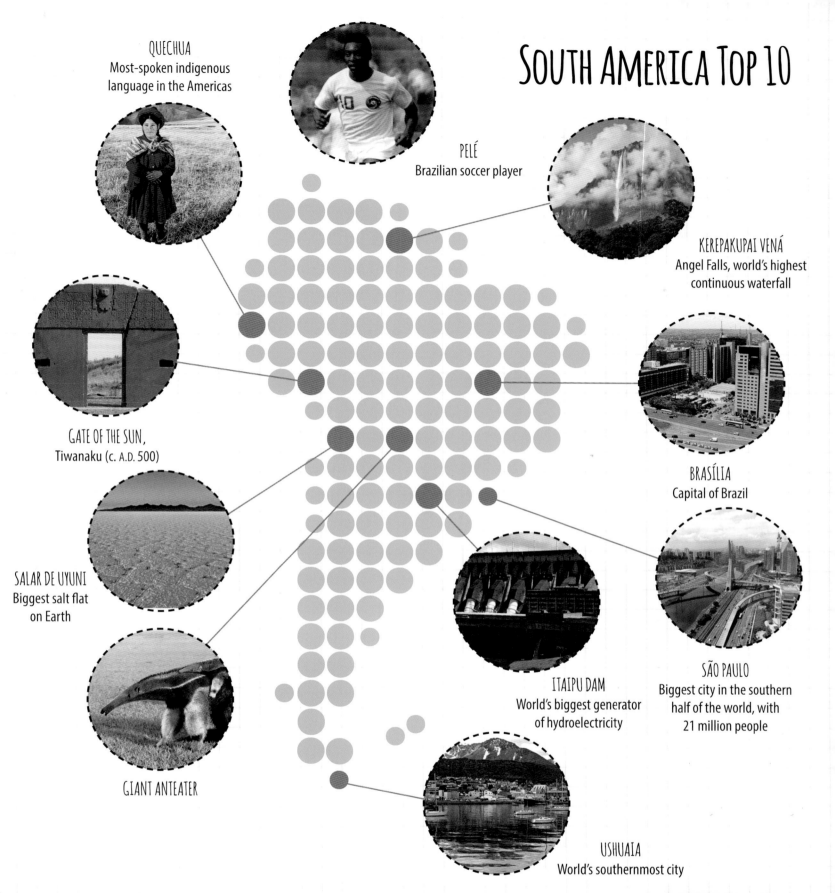

SOUTH AMERICA TOP 10

QUECHUA
Most-spoken indigenous language in the Americas

PELÉ
Brazilian soccer player

KEREPAKUPAI VENÁ
Angel Falls, world's highest continuous waterfall

GATE OF THE SUN,
Tiwanaku (c. A.D. 500)

BRASÍLIA
Capital of Brazil

SALAR DE UYUNI
Biggest salt flat on Earth

GIANT ANTEATER

ITAIPU DAM
World's biggest generator of hydroelectricity

SÃO PAULO
Biggest city in the southern half of the world, with 21 million people

USHUAIA
World's southernmost city

SOUTH AMERICAN HEADLINERS

In the 1800s the armies of **Simón Bolívar** (left) helped large areas of South America break away from rule by the Spanish empire. Brazilian **Chico Mendes** (1944–1988) campaigned to protect the Amazon rain forest. **Rigobeta Menchú** (born 1959) won the Nobel Peace Prize in 1992 and the Prince of Asturias Award in 1998 for her human rights work in Guatemala. South America's soccer superstars have included **Pelé** (born 1940), **Diego Maradona** (born 1960), and **Lionel Messi** (born 1987) (right).

Northern South America

Bolivia - Brazil - Colombia - Ecuador - French Guiana
Guyana - Peru - Suriname - Venezuela

Big cities rise from the Atlantic and Caribbean coasts. Gleaming, elegant skyscrapers tower over beaches and busy avenues. But clinging to the hillsides are *favelas,* or shanty towns, which are home to many poor people. In the northeast are the forests and rivers of the Guiana Highlands and the sugarcane and rice fields of the coast. In the northwest, the flooding Orinoco River spills out across the Llanos grasslands, where millions of cattle are herded by cowboys. Venezuela also has some of the world's biggest reserves of oil. In the west, the land rises through the mist to the high peaks of the Andes, where the air is cool and dry. The Pacific coast and the mountains, too, have seen civilizations rise and fall for thousands of years. Here are today's high-altitude cities, such as Bogotá, Quito, and La Paz, and beside the Pacific, Lima, and Callao.

RICH AND POOR, RIGHT NEXT DOOR
The huge statue of Christ the Redeemer looks out across Rio de Janeiro. Spread out below are the makeshift houses of the poor, the luxury apartments of the rich, the city's green hills, and the blue of the ocean.

MACHU PICCHU, CITY OF THE INCAS

GALÁPAGOS ISLANDS (ECUADOR)

PACIFIC OCEAN

CATTLE ROUNDUP IN THE MATTO GROSSO, BRAZIL

MACAWS IN THE AMAZON RAIN FOREST

SNUG! A BABY FROM OLLANTAYTAMBO, PERU

EQUATOR

VENEZUELA
Lake Maracaibo
CARACAS
Orinoco
Angel Falls
BOGOTÁ
COLOMBIA
QUITO
Ecuador
PERU
Andes
LIMA
Lake Titicaca
LA PAZ
BOLIVIA

GUYANA
GEORGETOWN
SURINAME
CAYENNE
Guiana Highlands
FRENCH GUIANA (FRANCE)

Amazon River basin
Amazon R.

BRAZIL

SALVADOR
Brazilian Highlands
BRASÍLIA
RIO DE JANEIRO
SÃO PAULO

RECORD BREAKERS

Kerepakupai Vená, or Angel Falls, in Venezuela is the world's highest uninterrupted waterful, tumbling **3,212 ft. (979 m)** • Lake Titicaca is another record breaker. It is **12,507 ft. (3,812 m)** high in the Andes Mountains, on the border between Bolivia and Peru. It is the highest lake on Earth to be navigated by big boats. (But the locals use canoes made from a kind of rush called totora) • The Galápagos Islands are home to the world's largest tortoises, with some exceeding **5 ft. (1.5 m)** in length and reaching 250 kg (550 lbs).

A DESERT MYSTERY

In Peru's Nazca Desert, there are 1,500-year-old lines scraped onto the surface. Some form patterns or pictures of monkeys, hummingbirds, and fish. They are gigantic and only make sense when seen from the air. Despite many theories, no one is really sure how they got there.

51

WHO LIVES HERE?

Who doesn't? It's quite a mix! In Brazil most people speak Portuguese. In Guyana they speak English. In Suriname it is Dutch, and in French Guiana, French. In the rest of the region, Spanish is the top language. But hundreds of other languages are spoken, too, because many people are descended from other **European, African, Asian, or indigenous "Indian"** peoples, such as the **Yanomami** of Brazil, the **Tukano** of Colombia, and the **Quechua** of the Andes.

Brazil is the largest country in all of South America: **3,287,597 sq. mi.** (8,515,767 km²)

Rio de Janeiro stages the world's most **spectacular carnival**, with glittering costumes and parades —and two million people out on the streets dancing the samba.

THE KIDS FROM THE BARRIO

In Colombia, a city neighborhood is called a *barrio*. About 10.8 million people live in the area around Bogotá. Many are poor people from the countryside. They've come to look for work but don't have enough money to buy a house or rent an apartment. They live in shacks made of odds and ends. The hillsides are covered in these homes.

Did you know that **mummies** didn't only come from ancient Egypt? They have also been found high in the **Andes**. Bodies were left in stone towers called chullpas and were preserved by the dry and cold air. Some were human sacrifices.

The hunters of the **Colombian rain forest** use poison darts to bring down wild animals. They collect the poison from a **gold-colored frog** that contains just 0.000035 oz. (1 mg) of a deadly toxin. This is enough to kill thousands of mice or 20 humans!

In **Peru and Ecuador,** make sure you wear **yellow** underwear on New Year's Eve. If you don't have any, buy them at any street stall.

Yellow means good luck in the year to come. Wear **red** ones if you want to fall in love!

Thanks to oil, **Venezuela** is the wealthiest country in South America.

"HELLO" IN THE QUECHUA LANGUAGE:
Napaykullayki

MAKING MUSIC:
Panpipes of the Andes

UNUSUAL FOOD:
Roasted "big-bottom" leafcutter ants (Colombia)

MOST PRECIOUS BIRD POOP:
The guanay cormorant from Peru produces valuable guano for fertilizer

SLOWEST MAMMAL ON EARTH:
The three-toed sloth

TRAFFIC CRAZINESS:
São Paolo has had traffic jams of 183 mi. (295 km)

MOST FIFA WORLD CUP WINS :
Brazil has won soccer's World Cup five times

THE TOOTHIEST LAND MAMMAL:
The giant armadillo has between 80 and 100 teeth

MOST LOGGED IN:
Brazil is the world's second-biggest user of Facebook and Twitter (after the U.S.)

Wake up and smell the coffee! Brazil produces the most coffee in the world—almost 3 million tons a year.

The railroad from Lima to Huancayo in Peru reaches **15,843 ft. (4,829 m)** above sea level—on track for the top of the world!

Southern South America

Argentina - Chile - Falkland Islands/Islas Malvinas
Paraguay - South Georgia - Uruguay

It's a tough ride on horseback across the Gran Chaco—a hot, dry plain that stretches into Paraguay. Most Paraguayans live in the eastern part of the country, which is easier to farm. In Uruguay cattle graze the hills and valleys, while farmers grow fruits and vegetables in the countryside near the Atlantic coast. Most Uruguayans live in Montevideo, a city on the north bank of the Rio de la Plata. On the south bank of the Plate is Buenos Aires, capital of Argentina. This country stretches west to fertile valleys and vineyards beneath the high Andes. The wide grassland region of the Pampas is cattle country and was once famous for its cowboys, known as Gauchos. The climate cools southward to Patagonia and its dry, windswept valleys. Between the Andes and the Pacific Ocean, Chile is the longest and thinnest country in this atlas. It has deserts, copper mines, vineyards and forests, ragged coastlines, and active volcanoes. Chile and Argentina both occupy Tierra del Fuego, at the chilly southern tip of the continent.

GREAT CHUNKS OF ICE!
Patagonia's Perito Moreno glacier is an awesome sight.
It is 19 mi. (30 km) long and 558 ft. (170 m) thick.

VALLEY OF THE MOON, ATACAMA DESERT, CHILE

CHILEAN VINEYARD

GOLDEN LION TAMARIN, BRAZIL

ANDEAN LLAMA, CHILE

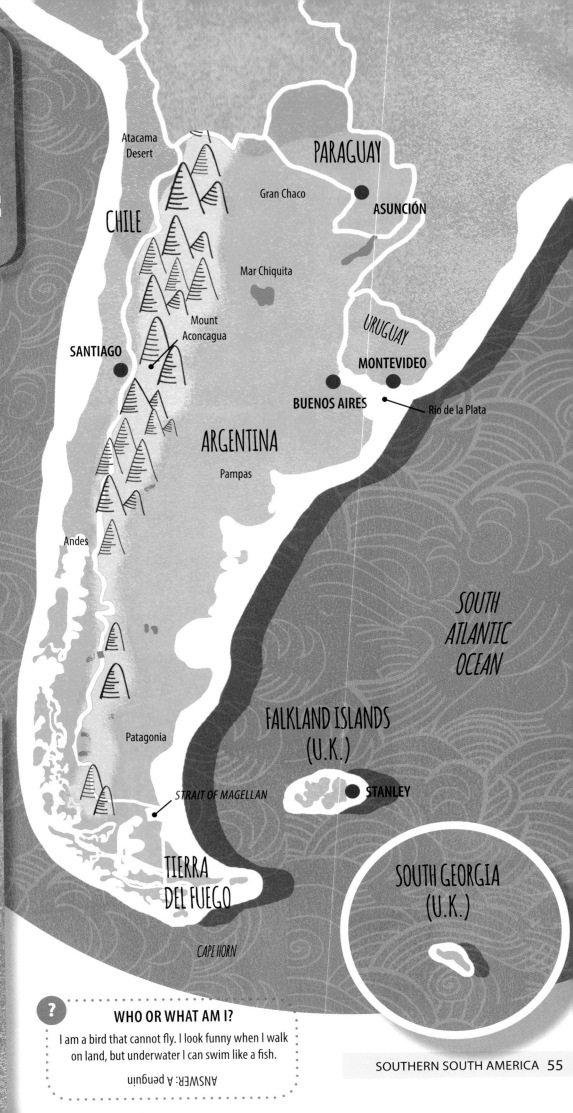

DRY AS A BONE
The driest and oldest hot desert on the planet is Chile's Atacama. In some parts it hasn't rained for hundreds of years! Some people say it looks like the surface of the planet Mars.

BUENOS AIRES

PACIFIC OCEAN

LANDS OF ICE AND FIRE
The Rio de la Plata (River Plate) is **140 mi. (220 km)** across at its mouth, making it the widest river in the world • Mount Aconcagua in the Argentine Andes is a double record breaker. It is the highest peak in the southern half of the world and is also the highest in the western part of the world. Its height? A dizzying **22,387 ft. (6,961 m)** above sea level • The rim of the Pacific Ocean is notorious for its earthquakes and volcanoes. Chile has **137** active volcanoes.

Atacama Desert

CHILE

PARAGUAY

Gran Chaco

ASUNCIÓN

Mar Chiquita

Mount Aconcagua

SANTIAGO

URUGUAY

MONTEVIDEO

BUENOS AIRES

Río de la Plata

ARGENTINA

Pampas

Andes

SOUTH ATLANTIC OCEAN

Patagonia

FALKLAND ISLANDS (U.K.)

STANLEY

STRAIT OF MAGELLAN

TIERRA DEL FUEGO

SOUTH GEORGIA (U.K.)

CAPE HORN

? WHO OR WHAT AM I?
I am a bird that cannot fly. I look funny when I walk on land, but underwater I can swim like a fish.

ANSWER: A penguin

WHO LIVES HERE?

The Indian peoples of the region include the **Guaraní**, the **Mataco**, and the **Mapuche.** The years of rule by Spain, beginning in the 1500s, mean that **Spanish** is still the main language today. All kinds of other immigrants came to settle here over the years— **Italians, Germans, Jews, Russians, Welsh, Poles, Syrians, Lebanese, Japanese, and Koreans.**

Argentina is the largest country in southern South America: **1,068,300 sq. mi.** (2,766,890 km²)

The **Andean condor** has a gigantic wingspan of up to **10.5 ft.** (3.2 m).

The **Drake Passage** between Cape Horn and Livingston Island in Antarctica is **just 503 mi. (809 km)** across.

A STORY OF HOPE

In 2010, 33 Chilean miners were trapped deep underground after a rock fall. One of them was named Ariel Ticona. While he was there, his wife gave birth to a baby girl. Ariel sent a message to the surface saying that she should be named Esperanza. That means "hope." Incredibly, the miners were rescued after 69 days.

In 2009 the **Uruguayan** government gave every school kid in the country a free laptop.

Probably the biggest dinosaur known to have existed was discovered in **Patagonia in 2014**. This titan was **131 ft. (40 m) long** and **66 ft. (20 m) tall**. It weighed about **80 tons**.

It was roughly the size and weight of a **Boeing 737**!

"HELLO" IN THE GUARANÍ LANGUAGE:
Mbaé'chepa

NATIONAL SIZZLER OF ARGENTINA:
Asado (beef barbecued in an outdoor pit)

BIGGEST CITY POPULATION:
Greater Buenos Aires—12.8 million

HARDEST TREE TO CLIMB:
Chile's national tree, the Chilean pine (also known as the monkey puzzle tree)

MOST DRAMATIC DANCE MOVES:
The tango, invented in Buenos Aires

NON-FLYING BIRD:
The rhea, a South American version of the ostrich, cannot fly at all

WHY DIDN'T THE CHICKEN CROSS THE ROAD?:
The 9 de Julio Avenue in Buenos Aires is the world's widest. It has seven lanes in each direction and two side roads of two lanes each!

Popular snack in **Peru**: *chifle*— fried and salted chips made of green or ripe plantain.

The voyage around Cape Horn is notorious. Fierce winds and 100 ft. (30 m) waves caused many wrecks in the days of the old sailing ships.

Almost **one-fifth** of all the fish caught in the world's seas come from the cold Humboldt current, which sweeps northward along the coast of **Chile and Peru.**

1/5

Europe

"Learn from yesterday, live for today, hope for tomorrow."

Albert Einstein

There are snowy northern forests, green fields, and woods full of wild flowers, moors, and heaths. There are awesome mountain ranges such as the Alps, as well as lowlands crossed by rolling rivers. There are olive groves, vineyards, and sunny beaches. Europe is not one of the bigger continents, but here you can meet all kinds of different peoples, hear many languages, and see a fantastic variety of landscapes.

To the north, Europe borders the icy Arctic Ocean. The Atlantic Ocean brings rain to western shores. Europe's sunny south meets the warm, blue waters of the Mediterranean and Black seas. The continent stretches eastward to the Caucasus and Ural mountains. Beyond lies Asia. In fact Europe and Asia together make up one mega landmass called Eurasia.

In addition to Europe's big modern cities you can still see prehistoric stone circles, beautiful cathedrals and castles from the Middle Ages, and factories and railroads from the industrial age of the 1800s. At that time European empires ruled large parts of the world, spreading languages such as Spanish, French, and English around the globe.

Five countries cross the divide between Europe and Asia—Russia, Turkey, Azerbaijan, Georgia, and Kazakhstan. They appear in the Asia section of this book.

MAP KEY
1 Portuguese fishing boat
2 Oranges 3 Mont Saint Michel,
France 4 Bagpipes 5 Stave church
6 Brandenburg Gate, Berlin
7 European bison 8 Painted eggs
9 Pelican 10 Greek windmill
11 Dolphin 12 Gondola, Venice
13 Duomo, Florence 14 Sagrada
Familia, Barcelona

Today 28 nations are linked as members of an international organization called the European Union (EU).

Area: 3,930,000 sq. mi. (10,180,000 km²)
Fact: sixth-largest continent
Population: 741.2 million

NORWAY
SWEDEN
FINLAND
DENMARK
ESTONIA
LATVIA
LITHUANIA
BELARUS
RUSSIA
BALTIC SEA
GERMANY
POLAND
Oder R.
Rhine R.
Danube R.
CZECH REPUBLIC
SLOVAKIA
LIECHTENSTEIN
AUSTRIA
HUNGARY
SLOVENIA
CROATIA
BOSNIA & HERZEGOVINA
SERBIA
UKRAINE
Dniester R.
MOLDOVA
ROMANIA
Dnieper R.
BLACK SEA
SAN MARINO
MONTENEGRO
KOSOVO
MACEDONIA
BULGARIA
TURKEY
ITALY
VATICAN CITY
ALBANIA
GREECE
Sardinia
Sicily
Crete

Exploring Europe

Fly into cities such as London, Paris, Rome, or Berlin, and you will see modern business districts built of steel and glass next to ancient buildings dating back hundreds or even thousands of years. You will see traditional ceremonies and festivals alongside the latest in fashion, art, and pop music. You can shop in shiny stores or busy street markets. There is often a lively coming together of cultures and peoples from around the world. There are suburbs, too, poorer areas and regions, industrial zones and seaports, and landscapes shaped by thousands of years of farming.

The **Scandinavian** Peninsula is about **1,150 mi. (1,850 km)** long

BUDAPEST ON THE DANUBE RIVER

GRIVOLA AND GRAND NOMENON MOUNTAINS, AOSTA VALLEY, ITALY

WHITE STORK

STEAM LOCOMOTIVE

Lands and seas

Western Europe is kept warm by an ocean current called the North Atlantic Drift, which keeps the climate mild • Eastern Europe is farther from the ocean and has greater extremes of hot and cold • "Mediterranean" means "in the middle of the land." This sea covers an area of about **965,000 sq. mi. (2.5 million km²)**.

Inventive Europe

Europe is famous for some amazing inventions. These include
• the thermometer **(c. 1593)**
• the newspaper **(1605)** • the telescope **(1608)** • the steam locomotive **(1803)**
• photography **(1822)** • the saxophone **(1846)** • the automobile **(1885)**
• the television **(1926)**
• ballpoint pens **(1938)**
• the World Wide Web **(1989)**.

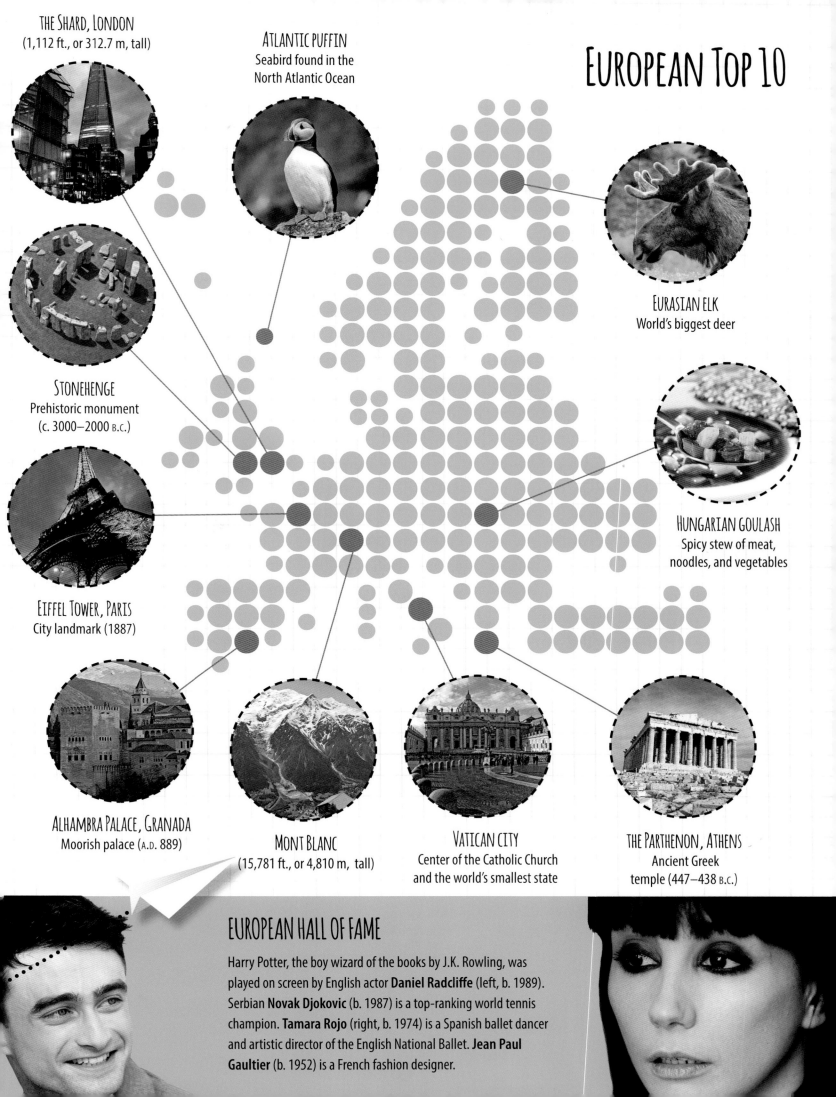

EUROPEAN TOP 10

THE SHARD, LONDON
(1,112 ft., or 312.7 m, tall)

ATLANTIC PUFFIN
Seabird found in the
North Atlantic Ocean

STONEHENGE
Prehistoric monument
(c. 3000–2000 B.C.)

EIFFEL TOWER, PARIS
City landmark (1887)

EURASIAN ELK
World's biggest deer

HUNGARIAN GOULASH
Spicy stew of meat,
noodles, and vegetables

ALHAMBRA PALACE, GRANADA
Moorish palace (A.D. 889)

MONT BLANC
(15,781 ft., or 4,810 m, tall)

VATICAN CITY
Center of the Catholic Church
and the world's smallest state

THE PARTHENON, ATHENS
Ancient Greek
temple (447–438 B.C.)

EUROPEAN HALL OF FAME

Harry Potter, the boy wizard of the books by J.K. Rowling, was
played on screen by English actor **Daniel Radcliffe** (left, b. 1989).
Serbian **Novak Djokovic** (b. 1987) is a top-ranking world tennis
champion. **Tamara Rojo** (right, b. 1974) is a Spanish ballet dancer
and artistic director of the English National Ballet. **Jean Paul
Gaultier** (b. 1952) is a French fashion designer.

Northern Europe

Denmark - Estonia - Finland - Iceland
Latvia - Lithuania - Norway - Sweden

You know you're way up near the arctic circle when the sky flashes green and pink with the northern lights, when it stays light all night at midsummer, and when it is dark during the days of midwinter. Welcome to Europe's far north.

Norway, Sweden, and Denmark are sometimes known as Scandinavia. This region include forests of spruce and birch, lakes, mountains, and deep sea inlets called fjords. Winters are snowy, but summers can be warm and sunny. The living is easier in the farms and cities of the south. Iceland is known for its volcanoes and hot springs, which provide heat and power for housing and greenhouses.

Across the Baltic Sea is Finland, another land of lakes and forests, with its capital of Helsinki. Estonia, Latvia, and Lithuania have historical links with Germany and Poland and were part of the Soviet Union (Russia) until 1991.

CROSS-COUNTRY SKIING, NORWAY

ICELAND
REYKJAVIK

ATLANTIC OCEAN

OFFSHORE WIND POWER, DENMARK

NORTHERN LIGHTS AS VIEWED FROM ICELAND

EURASIAN EAGLE OWL

NORWEGIAN SEA

Lapland

FAEROE ISLANDS (DENMARK)

FINLAND

TAMPERE

HELSINKI

NORWAY

SWEDEN

BALTIC SEA

TALLINN

OSLO

ESTONIA

STOCKHOLM

RIGA

GOTHENBURG

LATVIA

AARHUS

LITHUANIA

NORTH SEA

DENMARK

COPENHAGEN

VILNIUS

MALMÖ

KALININGRAD (RUSSIA)

STAVE CHURCH, NORWAY

Northern moneymakers

Fish from the North Sea
- Timber and paper from the forests
- Oil and gas from the North Sea
Danish wind turbines • Danish bacon and butter • Iceland's greenhouse produce • Cars and trucks
- Electronics

?

WHO OR WHAT AM I?
I sail in a longship, live in a longhouse, and have a long beard, a long sword, and a long, deadly ax—so watch out, you wimps!

ANSWER: A hairy old Viking

WHO LIVES HERE?

The Danes, Swedes, Norwegians, and Icelanders are all **Germanic** peoples and speak closely related languages. The **Sami, Finns, and Estonians** are also related. The Letts (Latvians) and the Lithuanians are **Baltic** peoples.

Reykjavik, Iceland is the world's northernmost national capital.

LOVE LEGO BRICKS

Lego bricks were first made in Denmark back in 1949. Since then about 560 billion bricks, parts, and figures have been manufactured. And where better to see them than at the Legoland theme park in Billund, Denmark, right next door to the original Lego factory?

Sweden is the biggest of the Nordic countries by area: **173,860 sq. mi.** (450,295 km²)

Many northern European countries have **festivals of light** during the dark days of midwinter. Swedish girls often wear a crown of glowing candles for **St. Lucy's Day** (December 13).

The famous Øresund road plus rail bridge connects with the Drogden tunnel to link the Danish capital, Copenhagen, with Malmö, Sweden.

All steamed up! There are more than **2 million** saunas in **Finland**.

An ancient rock carving from **Alta, Norway,** suggests that people were skiing here about **4,000 to 5,000 years ago.**

"HELLO" IN FINNISH:
Hei

SHORTEST PLACE NAME:
A fishing village called Å, in Norway's Lofoten Islands

BALTIC JEWELRY:
Amber is a fossil tree resin that appears yellow, brown, or orange

MAKING MUSIC:
The 1970s Swedish pop group Abba sold 380 million albums worldwide

BEST SELLER:
Books about Pippi Longstocking, a character created by Swedish author Astrid Lindgren, were translated into 64 languages

MIDNIGHT SUN:
At Noordkapp in Norway the Sun never sets from May 14 to July 15

VOLCANOES:
Iceland has more than 20 active volcanoes

Copenhagen's most famous tourist attraction is a statue of **the little mermaid**, from the 1837 tale by Hans Christian Andersen.

Iceland's parliament, or Althing, is one of the world's oldest. It was founded in **A.D. 930.**

IKEA is a Swedish company that has 349 furniture stores in 43 countries. It is said to use about 1 percent of the world's wood supply!

The Danes snack on over **100 million** hot dogs each year.

Did you know that the **Vikings** discovered **North America** almost **500 years** before Christopher Columbus?

Northwest Europe

Austria – Belgium – France – Germany – Liechtenstein – Luxembourg
Monaco – Netherlands – Republic of Ireland – Switzerland – United Kingdom

Atlantic breakers roll in to meet high cliffs on the west coast of Ireland, a land of green grass and low hills. Northern Ireland, along with England, Scotland, and Wales on the larger island of Great Britain, is part of the United Kingdom. Here you travel through rolling farmland, moors and highlands, small villages, historic market towns, and large, busy cities such as London.

England is linked to France by a train tunnel beneath the English Channel. A high-speed TGV train whisks you to Paris or southward through vineyards and river valleys to the warm and sunny Mediterranean coast and the little city-state of Monaco. High mountains occupy the southeastern France, part of the Alpine ranges. Switzerland, tiny Liechtenstein, and Austria are beautiful countries with rich histories and cultures.

Germany stretches from the Alps to the North and Baltic seas, crossed by great rivers such as the Rhine and the Elbe. Here are forests, heaths, mountains, and plains, with many large industrial cities as well as historic castles and traditional houses.

THE KING'S CASTLE
King Ludwig II of Bavaria had a thing about castles. In 1869 he set about building the ultimate fairy-tale castle. It was called Schloss Neuschwanstein, and today it is one of Germany's top tourist attractions.

TGV HIGH-SPEED TRAIN, FRANCE

RED DEER, SCOTLAND

BRANDENBURG GATE, BERLIN, GERMANY

Scotland

NORTH SEA

Northern Ireland

EDINBURGH

BELFAST

REPUBLIC OF IRELAND

DUBLIN

UNITED KINGDOM

Wales

England

CARDIFF

LONDON

ATLANTIC OCEAN

ENGLISH CHANNEL

NETHERLANDS

AMSTERDAM

HAMBURG

Elbe R.

BERLIN

GERMANY

BELGIUM

BRUSSELS

Rhine R.

FRANKFURT

PARIS

Seine R.

Loire R.

LUXEMBOURG

Danube R.

LIECHTENSTEIN

VIENNA

Alps

SWITZERLAND

Alps

AUSTRIA

FRANCE

Rhône R.

ZURICH

VADUZ

Alps

BORDEAUX

Pyrenees

MARSEILLE

MONACO

Corsica (France)

AJACCIO

WOMAN IN BRETON COSTUME, FRANCE

SUPER STATS

Monaco is the smallest country in the region, with an area of just over **0.8 sq. mi. (2 km²)**

• The Alps run across eight countries and include about 100 peaks higher than **13,123 ft. (4,000 m)**

• London is the biggest city in northwest Europe, with a population of more than **8.3 million**

• Austria's rivers and lakes mean that it can produce more than half of its electricity by hydropower.

SECRETS OF THE UNIVERSE

Deep beneath the French-Swiss border there is a huge underground tunnel called the Large Hadron Collider. This is where scientists send particles whizzing round at high speed until they smash into each other. It sounds like a fantastic game, but actually this is the world's biggest physics experiment.

67

WHO LIVES HERE?

The countries of northwest Europe grew up over hundreds of years from a patchwork of smaller states. A visitor might think of the nationalities as simply **French, German, Dutch, or Swiss,** but within the borders there are in fact many peoples—**Scots, Welsh, Bretons, Walloons, Flemings, Frisians, Swabians, Bavarians** . . . Even little Switzerland has four official languages (French, Swiss-German, Italian, and Romansh). Europe's historical overseas empires mean that many people are also descended from **African, Asian,** and **Caribbean** roots.

Mainland **France** is the largest country in northwest Europe: **212,935 sq. mi.** (551,500 km²)

A big wall used to run through the middle of Berlin, with armed guards and barbed wire. From 1961 it divided the eastern part of the city from the west. The **Berlin Wall** was a harsh symbol of the **Cold War,** when Germany was divided into two separate countries. In 1989 the wall was knocked down, and today Berlin is the capital of a united Germany.

HOW LOW CAN YOU GO?

Belgium, the Netherlands, and Luxembourg are sometimes collectively referred to as the Low Countries because they are situated in the low-lying delta of the Rhine.

Sunny or rainy, dry or muddy? Whatever the weather, English crowds love open-air music festivals such as **Glastonbury.** Britain has been a center of pop music and youth fashion ever since the 1960s.

"HELLO" IN THE IRISH LANGUAGE:
Dia dhuit

FASHION CAPITAL OF THE WORLD:
Paris, France

HOME OF THE WALTZ :
Vienna stages more than 200 grand balls each year, many in the Hofburg Imperial Palace

PUZZLING PASTIME:
Rolling cheese down a grassy hill, Gloucestershire, England

WITCHIEST PLACE :
The Harz Mountains, Germany, home to many myths and fairy tales

MOST FAMOUS CAR RACE:
The Monaco Grand Prix, a Formula 1 race through the streets of Monte Carlo

LONGEST PLACE NAME:
Llanfairpwllgwyngyllgogerychwyrn-drobwllllantysiliogogogoch, Wales

MOST DELICIOUS SWEETS:
Belgian chocolates

Britain's National Health Service employs more than **1.7 million** people.

The Dutch grow about **3 billion** tulip bulbs each year and export them around the world.

Luxembourg may be little, but its people are the second-biggest wealth creators in the world (after the Qataris).

About **27%** of the **Netherlands** is below sea level.

Germany produced **5.4 million** cars in 2013.

Sports invented in northwest Europe

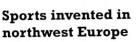

- **Golf** (Scotland)
- **Curling** (Scotland)
- **Cricket** (England)
- **Rugby** (England)
- **Soccer** (England)
- **Snooker** (England)
- **Hurling** (Ireland)
- **Gaelic football** (Ireland)
- **Real tennis/court tennis** (France)
- **Pétanque** (France)

Southwest Europe

Andorra - Balearic Islands - Gibraltar - Portugal - Spain

A big slab of land juts out from Europe into the Atlantic Ocean, below the stormy Bay of Biscay. This is the Iberian Peninsula, divided between Spain and Portugal. It is separated from France by the high mountains of the Pyrenees, where tourists visit the mini state of Andorra. Spain is rimmed by other mountains around the central, flat Meseta region.

Spain's northwest coast is green from Atlantic rains, but much of the country is dry and dusty. Spain can be sweltering hot in the summer. There are villages of small white houses, groves of orange and lemon trees, fields of sunflowers, and olive tree orchards. You can see castles and ornate Roman Catholic cathedrals, and in the south the Islamic palaces and fountains of the Moors, who ruled here in the Middle Ages. Madrid is the biggest city.

At Spain's southern tip, the great rock of Gibraltar is U.K. territory, just 9 mi. (14 km) from the coast of Africa. In Portugal there are river valleys, forests of cork oak, fishing villages and beaches by the Atlantic surf, and the historic port of Lisbon.

A VISION OF THE FUTURE
Is it a ship or a castle? No, it's a fantastic modern art gallery built out of stone, glass, and gleaming titanium. The Guggenheim Museum, Bilbao, lies in the Basque Country, Spain.

PICKING ORANGES, SPAIN

TOMATO-THROWING FESTIVAL NEAR VALENCIA, SPAIN

THE MONUMENT OF DISCOVERIES, LISBON, PORTUGAL

ATLANTIC
OCEAN

BAY OF
BISCAY

BASILICA OF THE SAGRADA FAMILIA, BARCELONA

Cantabrian Mts.

BILBAO

PORTO
Duro R.

PORTUGAL

SPAIN

ANDORRA

BARCELONA

Tagus R.

MADRID

BALEARIC ISLANDS

LISBON

VALENCIA

PALMA

Guadalquivir R.

Sierra Nevada

THE ROCK OF GIBRALTAR

SEVILLE

MEDITERRANEAN SEA

GIBRALTAR
(U.K.)

CAVE ART

At Altamira, in northern Spain, you can see amazing cave paintings of animals and hunters. They were made between about 13,000 and 17,000 years ago but look as if they were painted yesterday.

SUPER STATS

The Tagus is the longest river in the Iberian Peninsula, flowing **645 mi. (1,083 km)** through Spain and Portugal • The tallest mountain in Spanish territory is the volcanic Pico del Teide, in the Canary Islands off Africa's west coast, at **12,198 ft. (3,718 m)** • The Bay of Biscay is famous for its fierce winter storms • The population of greater Madrid is about **6.5 million**, making it the biggest urban area in southwest Europe.

WHO LIVES HERE?

The Spanish and Portuguese languages have spread around the world. The Iberian Peninsula has a patchwork of peoples and cultures. Some have their own languages or dialects. The **Catalans** live in the northeast, around Barcelona, as well as in Andorra and France. The Basque capital is Vitoria-Gasteiz. The **Basques** speak a language that is not related to any others in Europe.

There's no **tooth fairy** in Spain. Instead, they have a "tooth mouse" named Ratoncito Pérez!

IT'S FIESTA TIME!

Spain is famous for its countless festivals and pageants, for processions, parades, horseback cavalcades, dancing, and costumes. These celebrations may be rooted in history—in Roman Catholic religious rituals or in ancient regional customs— and they are often spectacular.

Spain is the largest country in southwest Europe: **212,935 sq. mi.** (505,370 km²)

Flamenco is a style of singing, guitar playing, and dancing popular in **southern Spain**. The dancers strut, shout, stamp, and clap. OLÉ!

Portuguese fishermen catch more sardines than any other kind of fish. Sardines freshly grilled?
"Sim, por favor!" (Yes, please!)

Patterned tiles in dazzling colors decorate the **Alhambra,** a fabulous Moorish palace in **Granada, Spain.**

THE SOUTHWEST EUROPE REAL DEAL!

TOURIST HOT SPOT:
About 53 million tourists visit Spain each year

"HELLO" IN EUSKARA [THE BASQUE LANGUAGE]:
Kaixo

AN AWESOME BREAKFAST:
Spanish doughnuts called churros, dipped in hot chocolate

STRANGEST LANGUAGE:
Silbo Gomero is a language of La Gomera on the Canary Islands that is made up entirely of whistles

EUROPE'S LONGEST BRIDGE:
Vasco da Gama Bridge, Lisbon, Portugal—10.7 mi. (17.2 km)

MOST POPULAR SOCCER TEAM IN WORLD:
Real Madrid (228 million fans)

"HELLO" IN SPANISH:
Hola

EUROPE'S BIG CAT:
The rare Iberian lynx

When the summer sun burns down at noon, the **Spanish** traditionally shut up shop and find a shady place for a **SIESTA,** or nap. Work starts up again later in the day when it gets cooler.

Spain produces over **41 percent** of the world's **olive oil.**

A riot of red! In **Buñol,** in the Valencia region of Spain, people gather each August to spend an hour throwing **150,000 squashed tomatoes** at each other.

Portugal is famous for its wines, fruit, and fish, but it is also a center for the IT, biotechnology, and aerospace industries.

Portugal and Spain produce over **90 percent** of the world's **corks.**

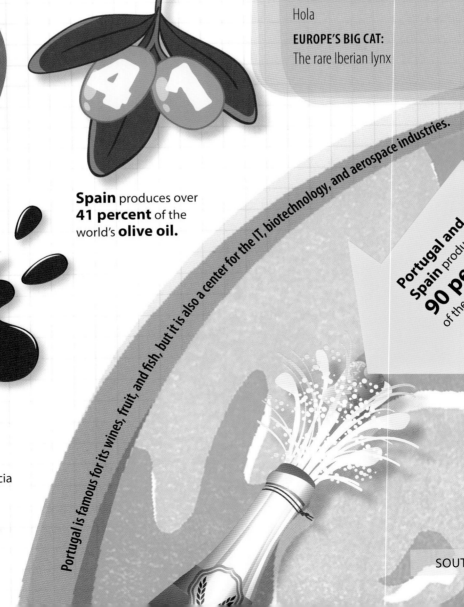

SOUTHEAST EUROPE

Albania - Bosnia & Herzegovina - Croatia - Greece - Italy
Kosovo - Malta - Montenegro - Republic of Macedonia
San Marino - Serbia - Slovenia - Vatican City

White doves flutter over red-tiled roofs. Fields form a patchwork across the fertile valley of the Po River. The city of Venice rises from a shimmering blue lagoon. In big, busy cities traffic swirls around ancient Roman ruins. This is Italy, a boot-shaped peninsula stretching from the Alps to the island of Sicily. The Apennine Mountains form a rocky backbone, north to south. The small island nation of Malta lies 176 mi. (284 km) off the coast of North Africa.

The broad Balkan Peninsula also extends into the Mediterranean Sea. Its northern lands include forests, limestone caves, fields of corn and sunflowers, and the sunny Adriatic coast. The small countries here were once united as a country called Yugoslavia, which broke up in the 1990s amid violence and war. Albania, a mountainous country to the north of Greece, is the poorest in the region.

The Balkan Peninsula ends in the mountains, plains, and ragged coastline of Greece. Ancient temples remind us that Greek civilizations shaped the culture of Europe. Scattered islands in sparkling blue seas are popular with tourists. The largest one is Crete.

ANCIENT DELPHI
About 2,400 years ago ancient Greek rulers came to the religious center of Delphi, on Mount Parnassus, to have their fortunes told.

THE DOLOMITES IN NORTHERN ITALY

MOSTAR BRIDGE IN BOSNIA & HERZEGOVINA

THE LEANING TOWER OF PISA, ITALY

Dolomite Mts.

ITALY

LJUBLJANA

SLOVENIA

SERBIA

Po R.

Danube R.

ZAGREB

BOSNIA & HERZEGOVINA

BELGRADE

CROATIA

MILAN

SARAJEVO

SAN MARINO

KOSOVO

Apennine Mts.

MONTENEGRO

SKOPJE

MACEDONIA

PODGORICA

ROME

VATICAN CITY

NAPLES

TIRANA

THESSALONIKI

ALBANIA

Sardinia

GREECE

ATHENS

PALERMO

Sicily

MEDITERRANEAN SEA

Crete

VALLETTA

MALTA

ETRUSCAN SCULPTURE, 400s B.C., ITALY

GREEK ORTHODOX PRIESTS, ATHENS

SUPER STATS

The awesome Roman empire was at its biggest in 117 B.C., when it covered about 1,930,511 sq. mi. (5 million km²)

• Vatican City State, the world headquarters of the Roman Catholic Church, is the smallest nation on Earth. It covers just 110 acres (44 ha) within the city of Rome

• Mount Olympus in Greece is 9,573 ft. (2,918 m) high. The ancient Greeks believed it was the home of the gods.

WHO LIVES HERE?

The Italian language has its origins in the **Latin** spoken in ancient Rome. The Maltese language is related to Arabic. Both Malta and Italy are **Roman Catholic** countries. Many peoples of the smaller Balkan states speak Slavic languages. They are mostly Christians, but some are Muslims, such as the **Bosniaks**. Many Albanians are Muslim, too. **Roma communities** are found across the region. The Greeks have their own language and alphabet, and many follow Greek Orthodox Christianity.

Italy is the largest country in the region: **116,348 sq. mi.** (301,340 km²)

ALBANIAN SCHOOLS

Albania is a country where many people are poor farmers, growing vegetables or olives. It is trying to improve its schools. A United Nations team has helped with rebuilding and repair and with providing much-needed libraries and laboratories.

The carnival in **Venice**, Italy, is famous for its elegant, mysterious masks.

At **Metéora** ("middle-of-the-air"), Greek Orthodox monasteries sit perched on pinnacles of rock 1,312 ft. (400 m) high. They date from the **Middle Ages.**

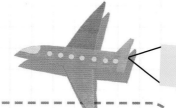

From mountaintop to seashore, Italy is home to more than **57,000 animal species**, one-third of the European total. They include wolves, brown bears, wild boar, and one of the tiniest mammals in the world, the Etruscan pygmy shrew—which weighs just **0.06 oz. (1.8 g).**

Rome's **Colosseum** once saw deadly gladiator fights and mock sea battles. It opened in **A.D. 80** and could hold up to **80,000** spectators.

"HELLO" IN ITALIAN:
Ciao

BIGGEST LAKE IN SOUTHERN EUROPE:
Skadar (Albania-Montenegro, 140-200 sq. mi., or 370-530 km² in surface area)

WORLD'S OLDEST SURVIVING REPUBLIC:
San Marino (founded A.D. 301)

BIG BANG:
Mount Etna in Sicily is Europe's highest active volcano

"THANK YOU" IN GREEK:
ευχαριστώ (pronounced "efcharistó")

MALTA'S ANCIENT MYSTERY:
Stone temples (c. 3600-3200 B.C.)

OLYMPIC GAMES:
Were held in southern Greece as early as 776 B.C.

FAVORITE SNACK IN ATHENS:
Koulouri (sesame bread ring)

FERRIES TO THE ISLANDS :
Piraeus, Greece, is Europe's busiest passenger port, with 20 million passengers a year

Greece exports tasty foods such as creamy yogurts, cheeses, olives and olive oil, honey, and melons.

Kosovo has the youngest population in Europe, with more than half of the people **under 25.**

Many names in the history of fast cars are **Italian**—Ferrari, Lamborghini, Alfa Romeo, Maserati . . .

Central Europe

Bulgaria - Czech Republic - Hungary - Poland - Romania - Slovakia

Gdansk is a Polish port on the Baltic Sea. Poland lies across the huge plain which stretches eastward into Russia, crossed by long rivers such as the Oder and the Vistula. Here are farms growing potatoes or beets, as well as forests, lakes, and industrial towns. In the middle is the busy capital city, Warsaw. Summers can be warm and winters very cold. Southern borders rise to the Sudeten and Tatra mountains.

The Czech Republic and Slovakia take in highlands, mountains, forests, and farms, as well as industrial and mining regions. Many visitors come to admire the beautiful old city of Prague. Another grand capital is Budapest, Hungary, on the banks of the Danube River. Hungary is a land of grassy plains, farms and orchards, forests, and mountains.

Romania lies to the north of the Danube, and the plains around Bucharest rise to form a great horseshoe of mountain ranges, known as the Carpathians and the Transylvanian Alps. Bulgaria takes up the northeastern part of the Balkan Peninsula, bordering Greece, Turkey, and the Black Sea.

IMPRESSIVE PRAGUE
The Czech city of Prague has been a center of learning, the arts, and politics for more than a thousand years.

STREET PERFORMER ON CHARLES BRIDGE, PRAGUE

PELICANS ON THE DANUBE DELTA

GDANSK

Vistula R.

POLAND

Oder R.

WARSAW

LODZ

KRAKOW

Tatra Mts.

PRAGUE

CZECH REPUBLIC

SLOVAKIA

BRATISLAVA

BUDAPEST

HUNGARY

Danube R.

Carpathian Mts.

ROMANIA

BUCHAREST

BLACK SEA

SOFIA

BULGARIA

WOODEN MONASTERIES, BÂRSANA, ROMANIA

DOWNTOWN WARSAW

SUPER STATS

Lake Balaton in Hungary is the biggest lake in Central Europe (**229 sq. mi., or 592 km²**) • Poland has 23 national parks, **1,269** nature reserves, and **100** bird sanctuaries • The People's Palace in Bucharest, Romania, is the largest civilian building in the world, covering **3,700,000 sq. ft. (340,000 m²)**. It has **1,100** rooms, **12** floors, and **4** underground levels, with another **4** under construction • The oldest golden treasure (**6,000 years old**) in the world was found in Bulgaria.

SPARKLING GLASS

You need some puff to blow glass in the old-fashioned way. Fine glass has been made in the historical Czech region of Bohemia since the Middle Ages. The region is still famous for its crystal glassware.

?

WHO OR WHAT AM I?

I can be blue, brown, silver, or green, and I travel a long, long journey from Germany through Central Europe to the Black Sea.

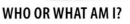
ANSWER: The Danube River

WHO LIVES HERE?

The region includes Catholic, Protestant, and Orthodox Christians, as well as Muslims and Jews. The **Poles, Czechs, Slovaks,** and **Bulgarians** are all **Slavic** peoples with their own languages. The **Hungarians,** also known as Magyars, are a separate ethnic group. So are the **Romanians,** whose language comes from the Latin of the old Roman empire. Many other peoples live in the region, including the **Roma**—who are not the same people as the Romanians.

Let's dance the **polka**! This lively folk dance from **Central Europe** conquered the world's ballrooms in the 1800s and is still popular today.

STEW-PENDOUS!

In Hungary they call their national dish *Gulyásleves* ("herdsman's soup"), but it is also popular across Central Europe and is known in English as goulash. It is a spicy beef stew seasoned with paprika, herbs, and garlic, and it may include vegetables such as diced potatoes. It's a winter warmer!

Poland is the largest country in Central Europe: **120,728 sq. mi.** (312,685 km²)

All lit up with Christmas decorations— St. Stephen's Basilica in Budapest, the capital of Hungary.

The element polonium is named after Poland, the native country of scientist Marie Sklodowska Curie, who discovered the element in 1898.

THE CENTRAL EUROPE REAL DEAL!

"HELLO" IN CZECH:
Ahoj!

HIGH TATRAS:
Slovakia's highest point is Gerlachovsky Stit, in the Tatra Mountains (8,711 ft., or 2,655 m)

WILD MUSHROOMS:
Every fall Central Europeans head to the woods to search for tasty mushrooms

SCENT OF ROSES:
Bulgaria produces 70 percent of all the world's rose oil, used in making perfumes

HOT SPRINGS:
Hungary has more than 1,000 hot springs and spas

FISH FOR CHRISTMAS:
In the Czech Republic, carp is the favorite choice for dinner on Christmas Eve

A SALT CATHEDRAL:
An underground cathedral is carved out of rock salt in Poland's Wieliczka Salt Mine

Millions of **doughnuts** called *paczki* are eaten by **Poles** on the last Thursday before the Christian fast of Lent.

Slovakia's industry is based on the manufacture of cars, televisions, and computer monitors.

The Masurian region of **northern Poland** has over **2,000 lakes**, linked by a maze of canals and rivers. It's popular for yachting, kayaking, and swimming in the summer.

The novel **Dracula** (1897) tells the tale of a **vampire** from Transylvania. The character may be based on a real-life prince from Romania called **Vlad the Impaler.** He lived in the 1400s.

Hungary is famous for its **horse** breeds and its **daredevil riders.**

Eastern Europe

Belarus - Moldova - Ukraine

Let's travel east to the borders of Russia. Trains bound for Moscow from Berlin or Warsaw will take you via the industrial city of Minsk, the capital of Belarus. Belarus is a low-lying, flat land with forests, marshes, and lakes.

To the south is Ukraine. Its capital, Kyiv or Kiev, looks out over the Dnieper River, and more than three million people live in or around the city. In the south the steppes (prairies) have a rich black soil known as chernozem. It is perfect for growing wheat, so this region is known as one of the world's big "bread baskets." The southern part of the country is warm, bordering the Black Sea around the port of Odessa. Westward, along the Dniester River, is the small country of Moldova, with its capital of Chisinau.

All three countries have in the past been part of the Russian empire or the Soviet Union. In the 1990s they broke away to become independent. Some of their peoples still wanted close ties with Russia, while others wanted to join up with Central and Western Europe. This has led to some big political problems.

KHOTYN FORTRESS AND DNIESTER RIVER, UKRAINE

ST. MICHAEL'S MONASTERY, KIEV

GRAIN HARVEST ON THE STEPPES

A PEBBLY BEACH ON THE BLACK SEA

MINSK

BELARUS

WORLD WAR II MEMORIAL, MINSK

KIEV

KHARKIV

Dnieper R.

UKRAINE

Dniester R.

MOLDOVA

ODESSA

CHISINAU

SEA OF AZOV

Crimea

BLACK SEA

BISON SANCTUARY
The ancient Bialowieza forest is on the border between Belarus and Poland. A home has been created there for the very rare European bison.

SUPER STATS
The Dnieper River flows through Russia, Belarus, and Ukraine on its **1,333 mi. (2,145 km)** journey to the Black Sea • The Eurasian Steppe stretches all the way from Moldova and Ukraine through Central Asia to Siberia • Wildlife of the steppes includes hamsters and ground squirrels • Moldova is the smallest—and poorest—country in Eastern Europe • **40 percent** of Belarus is covered by forest.

GOLDEN ORIOLE, MOLDOVA

? WHO OR WHAT AM I?
I am Europe's biggest rodent and have a broad, flat tail. I build dams and canals in lakes and rivers.

ANSWER: A Eurasian beaver.

WHO LIVES HERE?

Eastern Europe is the original homeland of the **Slavic peoples**, and today they make up the majority of the population. They include **Belarussians, Russians, Ukrainians,** and **Poles**. Some **Tartars**, of Turkic descent, live in Ukraine, and the Moldovans include ethnic **Romanians** and **Roma**. There are followers of Eastern Orthodox Christianity and also some Roman Catholics and Protestants.

Odessa is an important naval base, oil terminal, and seaport. But to many Ukrainians, Russians, and other Eastern Europeans, it's simply where they go on **vacation**. Days are spent sunbathing on the sunny beaches or wading in the Black Sea.

STREET TRADERS

Coming up with the goods . . . Across Eastern Europe you can buy almost anything at one of the numerous street markets. People like to haggle over the price of everything, from spare parts for their cars to batteries, sunglasses, watches, clothes with fake designer labels, pickles, potatoes, and fresh fruit.

The **Dnieper River** is the fourth-longest in Europe, at **1,420 mi.** (2,290 km)

Nested, or stacking, **matryoshka dolls**, Odessa, Ukraine. The more matryoshkas there are in a stack, the more expensive they are. Some commercial matryoshka sets have as many as 20 dolls.

Modern Minsk— this city landmark houses the Belarussian national library.

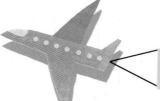

Moldova is one of only three countries whose **national flags** differ depending on which side you're looking at. (The other two are Paraguay and Saudi Arabia.)

SOUP OF THE DAY:
Borscht (beet soup)

FAVORITE SPORT:
The national sport in Moldova is traditional wrestling, known as trynta

ICE IS NICE:
In Belarus ice hockey is the most popular spectator sport

ABANDONED CITY:
Pripyat, Ukraine, has been sealed off ever since a disaster at the Chernobyl nuclear power plant in 1986

DEEP STATION:
Arsenalna in Kiev is the world's deepest underground train station, plunging 346 ft. (106 m)

THE BLACK STORK:
Is the national bird of Moldova

FRESH FROM THE FOREST:
Belarussians like a drink made from birch sap

At **Easter, Ukrainians** use wax and dyes to prepare eggs colored with fancy designs. They even have a special **Easter egg** museum in the city of Kolomyia—partly housed inside a giant **Easter egg**, of course!

Belarus has about **11,000 lakes**. The biggest is Lake Narach, **31 sq. mi. (80 km²)**.

On the move: Ukraine builds buses, trucks, streetcars, tractors, cars, ships, and aircraft.

Ukraine grows sunflowers and is the **world's** biggest producer of oil made from the seeds.

. . . it is also **Europe's** top producer of **honey.**

Moldovan monks in the **1200s** built an amazing cave monastery in the cliff face at Orheiul Vechi.

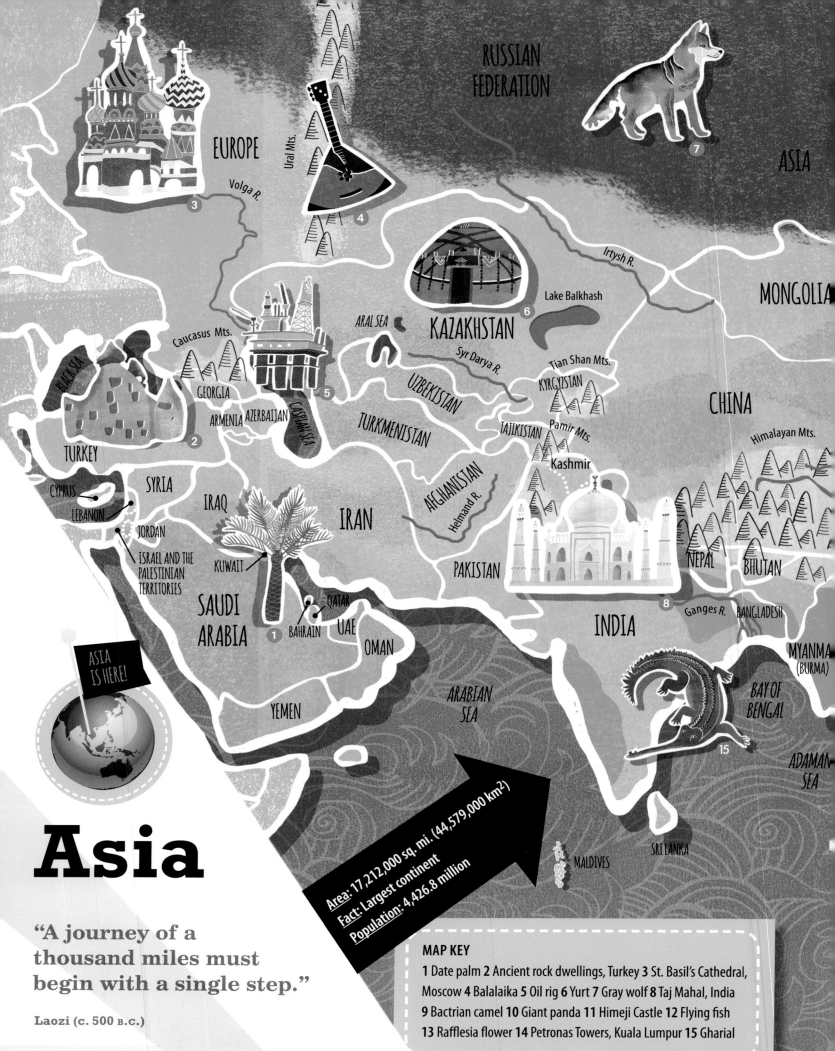

Asia

"A journey of a thousand miles must begin with a single step."

Laozi (c. 500 B.C.)

Area: 17,212,000 sq. mi. (44,579,000 km²)
Fact: Largest continent
Population: 4,426.8 million

MAP KEY
1 Date palm **2** Ancient rock dwellings, Turkey **3** St. Basil's Cathedral, Moscow **4** Balalaika **5** Oil rig **6** Yurt **7** Gray wolf **8** Taj Mahal, India **9** Bactrian camel **10** Giant panda **11** Himeji Castle **12** Flying fish **13** Rafflesia flower **14** Petronas Towers, Kuala Lumpur **15** Gharial

EUROPE
RUSSIAN FEDERATION
ASIA
Ural Mts.
Volga R.
Irtysh R.
MONGOLIA
Lake Balkhash
ARAL SEA
KAZAKHSTAN
Caucasus Mts.
Syr Darya R.
Tian Shan Mts.
KYRGYZSTAN
CHINA
GEORGIA
UZBEKISTAN
Pamir Mts.
BLACK SEA
ARMENIA AZERBAIJAN
TURKMENISTAN
TAJIKISTAN
Kashmir
Himalayan Mts.
TURKEY
CYPRUS
SYRIA
AFGHANISTAN
LEBANON
IRAQ
IRAN
Helmand R.
JORDAN
ISRAEL AND THE PALESTINIAN TERRITORIES
KUWAIT
PAKISTAN
NEPAL
BHUTAN
QATAR
SAUDI ARABIA
BAHRAIN
UAE
INDIA
Ganges R.
BANGLADESH
OMAN
MYANMA (BURMA)
ASIA IS HERE!
ARABIAN SEA
BAY OF BENGAL
YEMEN
ADAMAN SEA
MALDIVES
SRI LANKA

Siberia

Lake Baikal

SEA OF
OKHOTSK

9

NORTH
KOREA

SEA OF
JAPAN

SOUTH
KOREA

JAPAN

10

Yangtze R.

11

This is the biggest continent on the planet—in every sense. It has the most people, speaking 2,322 different languages. It reaches from the Arctic Ocean to far below the equator. In the west, Asia borders the Mediterranean Sea, and in the east the Bering Strait, just 51 mi. (82 km) from the U.S. state of Alaska. What's more, it is just part of an even bigger landmass called Eurasia. Europe lies to the west, beyond Russia's Ural Mountains.

Be prepared for anything. Asia has deep-frozen treeless tundra, deep forests of spruce and birch, farmland and plains, windy grasslands, and the highest mountains on Earth. It has hot deserts and frozen deserts, tangled tropical forests, and flooding river deltas. Its eastern shores make up the rim of the Pacific Ocean, a danger zone for earthquakes and volcanoes that is known as the "Ring of Fire."

Across Asia there are big differences between life in the country and life in the town, between rich and poor, young and old, and between tradition and the latest new technologies.

12

SOUTH
CHINA
SEA

PHILIPPINES

LAOS

THAILAND

VIETNAM

CAMBODIA

BRUNEI

MALAYSIA

SINGAPORE

INDONESIA

PACIFIC OCEAN

14

13

Five countries cross the divide between Asia and Europe—Russia, Turkey, Azerbaijan, Georgia, and Kazakhstan. They appear in this section of this book.

Awesome Asia

On top of a hill outside Kathmandu, Nepal, there is a Buddhist temple called Swayambhunath. Monkeys climb over its walls. Colored flags flutter in the breeze. Painted on the pinnacle are the eyes of the Buddha, looking out to the north, south, east, and west. A bird flying north from here would cross the Himalaya Mountains, the Tibetan Plateau, and the vast expanses of Siberia. A flight southward would cross the Ganges River and India's dusty plains. Far to the east the bird might follow the winding course of the Yangtze (Chang) River all the way to the East China Sea. To the west lies the valley of the Indus River, and beyond, the deserts of the Middle East.

RUB' AL'KHALI (THE EMPTY QUARTER), SAUDI ARABIA

THAILAND'S PHI PHI LEH ISLAND

Japan's highest peak is **Mount Fuji,** at 12,388 ft. (**3,776 m**) above sea level—and it's an active volcano!

INDIAN GREAT HORNBILL

Big geography

Asia's longest river? The Yangtze, at **3,915 mi. (6,300 km)**. That's number three in the world • Asia's biggest desert is the Gobi, in Mongolia and China, covering an area of **500,000 sq. mi. (1,295,000 km²)** • Asia's biggest island is Borneo, at **288,869 sq. mi. (748,168 km²)**.

BUDDHA STATUE

Cradle of religions

Many of the world's great religious faiths have their origins in Asia: the Baha'i faith, Buddhism, Christianity, Confucianism, Daoism, Hinduism, Islam, Jainism, Judaism, Shinto, and Sikhism.

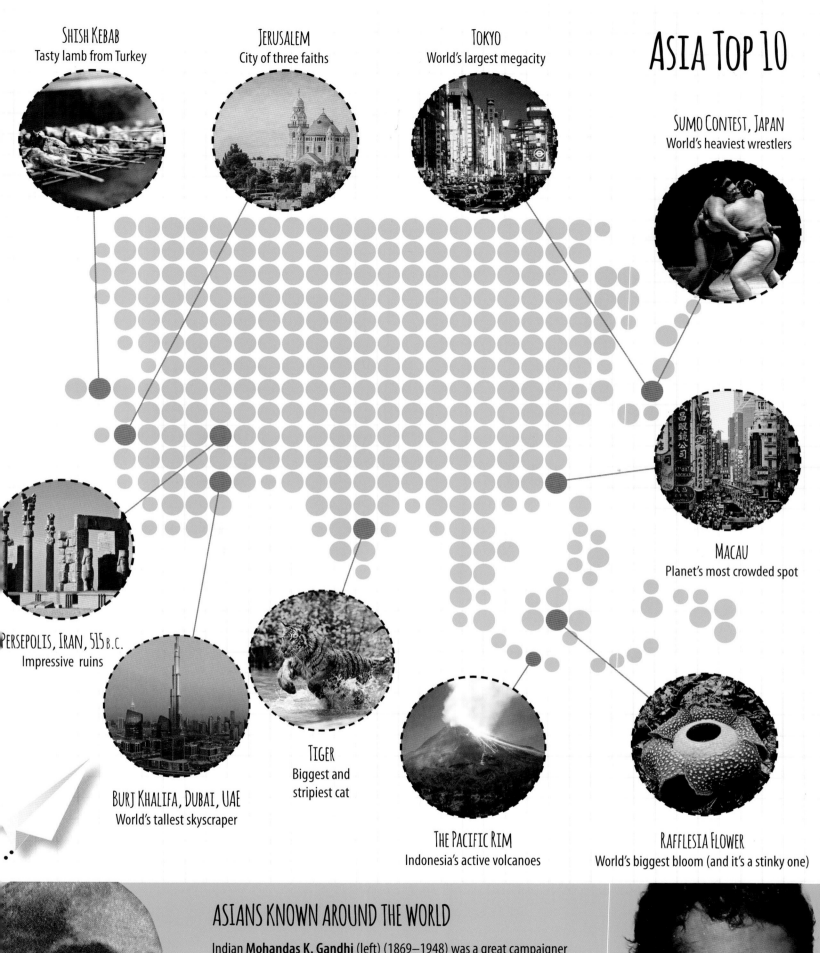

SHISH KEBAB
Tasty lamb from Turkey

JERUSALEM
City of three faiths

TOKYO
World's largest megacity

SUMO CONTEST, JAPAN
World's heaviest wrestlers

PERSEPOLIS, IRAN, 515 B.C.
Impressive ruins

MACAU
Planet's most crowded spot

BURJ KHALIFA, DUBAI, UAE
World's tallest skyscraper

TIGER
Biggest and stripiest cat

THE PACIFIC RIM
Indonesia's active volcanoes

RAFFLESIA FLOWER
World's biggest bloom (and it's a stinky one)

ASIANS KNOWN AROUND THE WORLD

Indian **Mohandas K. Gandhi** (left) (1869–1948) was a great campaigner for freedom and nonviolence. **Ban Ki-moon** (b. 1944), from South Korea, has served as secretary-general of the United Nations since 2007. **Liu Yang** (b. 1978) became China's first female astronaut in 2012. Indian **Sachin Tendulkar** (right) (b. 1973) is one of the greatest cricket players of all time.

ST. PETERSBURG

Ural Mts.

Irtysh R.

Volga R.

MOSCOW

NIZHNY NOVOGORO

CASPIAN SEA

Caucasus Mts.

BLACK SEA

GEORGIA **TBILISI**

ARMENIA

AZERBAIJAN

YEREVAN **BAKU**

NAKHCHIVAN ENCLAVE (AZERBAIJAN)

CEILING OF ORTHODOX CHRISTIAN CHURCH, ST. PETERSBURG

RUSSIA AND ITS NEIGHBORS

ARMENIA – AZERBAIJAN – GEORGIA – RUSSIAN FEDERATION

When the Sun is rising over Russia's Pacific coast, it is setting over its western borders. St. Petersburg, on the Gulf of Finland, is a fine city, but Russia's capital is Moscow. This large, sprawling city is built around a medieval fortress called the Kremlin. Moscow is the center of business, but much of Russia's wealth lies under the ground in Siberia, in the form of natural gas or metal ores.

Leave Moscow's Yaroslavsky station on the Trans-Siberian Express. You pass through the Ural Mountains into Asia, and for a whole week this huge country seems to rush by your window—sunshine and snow, endless forests, villages, grimy industrial cities, frozen lakes, and rivers. The train can take you to Vladivostok, or turn south into Mongolia, China, or North Korea.

In 1991 many regions of Russia, then known as the Soviet Union, became independent. You can see three of them on this map. Beyond the Caucasus Mountains, Georgia borders the Black Sea and mountainous Armenia, while oil-rich Azerbaijan borders the Caspian Sea.

ST. BASIL'S CATHEDRAL RED SQUARE, MOSCOW, BESIDE THE KREMLIN

Siberia

SEA OF OKHOTSK

Kamchatka Peninsula

KRASNOYASK

Lake Baikal

IRKUTSK

ICEBREAKERS OPEN ROUTES TO THE ARCTIC PORTS

MOSCOW'S BUSINESS DISTRICT

VLADIVOSTOK

Take a look at how huge Russia is! The world's biggest country covers one-eighth of Earth's surface. You can see here just how far north it stretches—all the way to the arctic circle.

Ukraine

Russia

Kazakhstan

Mongolia

China

ANCIENT LANDS

With an area of more than **3,727,044 sq. mi.** (9,653,000 km²), Siberia makes up roughly three-fourths of the total area of Russia • The Armenian capital, Yerevan, is an ancient city—it was founded in **782 B.C.** • The first known fireplace and construction in human history, which is dated back to **500,000 to 700,000** years ago…, was discovered in Azikh Cave, the largest cave in Azerbaijan.

ON TRACK

The Trans-Siberian is the world's longest railroad, covering 5,722 mi. (9,289 km) of track from Moscow to the Sea of Japan. It is a part of a wider network and crosses two continents and no fewer than eight time zones.

? **WHO OR WHAT AM I?**
I am big, brown, and furry—and an emblem of Russia itself!

ANSWER: Eurasian brown bear

WHO LIVES HERE?

Eight out of 10 people are ethnic Russians, who are **Slavs**. The chief language is Russian, written in its own alphabet (Cyrillic). Russia is a federation of regions and peoples. They include other Slavs such as ethnic **Ukrainians** and **Belarussians;** Siberian and arctic peoples; and Turkic groups such as the **Tatars, Bashkir,** and **Chuvash.** About 40 percent of Russians follow the Eastern Orthodox form of Christianity, while almost 7 percent are Muslims. The countries to the south are home to **Georgians, Azeris, Armenians,** and many others.

High leaps and **kicks** put drama into dances performed by the **Cossack** communities of southern Russia and Ukraine.

THE FIRST BELL

It's the first day of fall in Russia, September 1. It is the beginning of the new school year, too. It is called Knowledge Day. Students are dressed up and carry bunches of flowers to give to their new teachers. One of the youngest students is carried around the school ringing "the first bell" of the year.

Russia, in both Europe and Asia, is the biggest country in the world: **6,592,800 sq. mi.** (17,098,246 km²)

Many of the world's greatest **ballet dancers** have come from Russia.

St. Petersburg's State Hermitage Museum contains more than **3 million** precious items.

Between 1885 and 1917 **Peter Carl Fabergé** made 54 jeweled Easter eggs for the Russian royal family. Today they are worth **zillions of roubles!**

CHECK MATE!:
Russia has produced many chess grand masters

WHITE NIGHTS:
Midsummer party time in St. Petersburg

RARE SPOTTED CAT:
The magnificent snow leopard

RUSSIAN SPRING FESTIVAL:
Maslenitsa—pancakes, sleigh rides, bonfires

HIGHEST PEAK IN RUSSIA:
Mount Elbrus (18,510 ft., or 5,642 m)

WORLD'S BIGGEST INLAND SEA:
Caspian Sea—143,200 sq. mi. (371,000 km²)

MOST ANCIENT CHRISTIAN STATE:
Armenia (since A.D. 301)

In 2012 a **39,000-year-old woolly mammoth** (ice age elephant) was found deep frozen in the soil of Siberia.

The longest river system is the **Yenisei-Angara-Selenge,** at **3,445 mi.** (5,539 km). Horse trotting races are held on the deep frozen river in the winter.

Mineral fuels, such as oil, account for almost 60 percent of Russia's exports, but it also exports iron, steel, and precious metals.

How would you like to live in the village of Oymyakon in Siberia? It once recorded a winter temperature of **−89.9°F (−67.7°C).** But in the summer the temperature has been known to reach **94°F (34.6°C).**

Lake Baikal is the world's deepest lake, at **5,387 ft.** (1,642 m). It contains about **20 percent** of all the unfrozen freshwater in the world. It is about **25 million years old.**

Central Asia

Afghanistan – Kazakhstan – Kyrgyzstan – Tajikistan – Turkmenistan – Uzbekistan

Central Asia lies at the crossroads of the continent, on the ancient trading routes known as the Silk Road. To the north is Siberia, across the Irtysh River. To the east the high Pamir and Tian Shan ranges form a mountain wall with China. To the west is the Caspian Sea and Iran. Afghan buses and trucks must make a steep descent down the Kabul Gorge before heading south to the Khyber Pass and Pakistan.

Central Asia is a land of steppe grasslands, deserts, and plateaus, crossed by pickups, other trucks, horses, or Bactrian camels. It's a harsh landscape, and it can be bitterly cold or desperately hot.

The region is rich in oil and minerals, but for many it is a hard life picking cotton for low wages in Uzbekistan or Kazakhstan. Life can be even tougher in Afghanistan, where there have been long periods of war.

The five northern countries were once part of the Soviet Union, as Russia was then known, but became independent in 1991.

GALLOPING TACTICS! THE GAME OF BUZKASHI

CHAR MINAR, BUKHARA, UZBEKISTAN

A YURT ON THE KYRGYZ STEPPE

THE SILK ROAD LED FROM CHINA TO CENTRAL ASIA AND BEYOND

PEAKS OF THE TIAN SHAN, KYRGYZSTAN

ASTANA ●

KAZAKHSTAN

Lake Balkhash

Irtysh R.

ARAL SEA

Syr Darya R.

BISHKEK ●

UZBEKISTAN

KYRGYZSTAN

Tian Shan Mts.

CASPIAN SEA

TASHKENT ●

Karakum
Desert

TURKMENISTAN

DUSHANBE ●

TAJIKISTAN

Pamir Mts.

ASHKHABAD ●

KABUL ●

AFGHANISTAN

Helmand R.

SUPER STATS

The region's biggest city is Kabul,
the capital of Afghanistan, which has a
population of **3.5 million** • The highest
peak in this mountainous part of Asia is
Ismail Somoni in Tajikistan, at
24,590 ft. (7,459 m) • About
70 percent of Turkmenistan is taken
up by the Karakum Desert.

THE SEA THAT VANISHED

Rusting ships lie on dry land. The Aral Sea
was once the fourth-biggest lake in the
world. When water was piped off to irrigate
crops, the sea shrank to one-tenth of its size,
leaving behind a salty, polluted desert.

? **WHO OR WHAT AM I?**

I have two humps and a shaggy
coat to keep me warm.

ANSWER: Bactrian camel.

WHO LIVES HERE?

Peoples of Central Asia have given the modern countries their names —the **Turkmen, Kazakhs, Uzbeks, Kyrgyz,** and **Tajiks.** The **Uyghurs** live on both sides of the Chinese border. In Afghanistan there are other groups as well, such as the **Pashtun, Balochi, Hazara,** and **Aimaq.** Dari, a form of Persian, is spoken in western Afghanistan. The religion of the region is Sunni Islam. Many Muslim women in Afghanistan wear a full robe and veil, called a chadri.

A deep blue stone called **lapis lazuli** has been mined in Afghanistan for about **8,000 years.** It is made into fantastic jewelry.

Kazakhstan is the largest country in the world with no access to the ocean: **1,059,039 sq. mi.** (2,742,900 km²)

Where the **space age** began: Kazakhstan's **Baikonur Cosmodrome** (run by Russia) is the world's first and largest space launch site.

KALEIDOSCOPE OF COLOR

At a yard-dying factory in Kabul, men hang woolen yarn out to dry. The colors are rich reds, oranges, and purples. They will be used for making carpets with wonderful designs and patterns. For hundreds of years Afghanistan and other countries of Central Asia have been making rugs and carpets of the highest quality.

All the "stans"...
"-stan" means "place of," "country," or "land" in the **Persian language.**

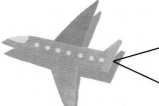

One of the world's finest and most ancient **horse** breeds comes from **Turkmenistan**. The Akhal-Teke is famous for its speed, its staying power, its intelligence—and its glossy coat.

MARE'S MILK DRINK:
Kumiss, popular with the Kazakhs and Kyrgyz

THE YURT:
Round felt tent of the Steppe nomads . . . Cozy in the cold!

THE MARKHOR:
Is a wild goat with huge corkscrew horns

CRAZIEST SPORT:
Afghan buzkashi, a wild horseback contest which can go on for several days

WEIRDEST NOSE:
The saiga antelope has a big, flexible nose, which is partly dust filter and partly air conditioner

THE ROAD TO SAMARKAND :
In Uzbekistan—it is the most famous city on the old Silk Road

Favorite **Afghan dish**: kabuli palaw—rice, lentils, nuts, raisins, carrots, and lamb.

The tomb of the **golden man** was found in Issyk in Kazakhstan. He was a Scythian **prince** from about 2,300 years ago. His coat was decorated with more than **3,000 pieces of gold.**

Kazakhstan has the top economy of Central Asia. It exports oil, metals, and wheat.

It's a nutty place! **Kyrgyzstan** is famous for its **almonds, pistachios,** and **walnuts.**

There are **158** named mountain ranges in **Kyrgyzstan.** The highest peak in the Tian Shan, on the Chinese border, is Jengish Choqusu, at **24,046 ft.** (7, 439 m).

East Asia

China - Japan - Mongolia - North Korea - South Korea

China is ringed by the world's highest mountains. In the west is the Tibetan Plateau, the "roof of the world." Long rivers such as the Yangtze (Chang) wind eastward. Most Chinese people live in the east or south, harvesting wheat, corn, or rice on the plains, or seeking work in crowded new megacities. Chinese civilization dates back over 3,000 years, but these days everything in China is changing fast.

Hong Kong and Macau are Special Administrative Regions of China. The island of Taiwan is claimed by China but has its own government.

Mongolia, too, is changing, with new coal mines and factories. Wind, scorching heat, or severe frosts blast your face as you travel through the empty deserts and grasslands. Here and there you see the tents, or gers, of sheep herders, a 4 x 4, and galloping horses kicking up dust.

The Korean Peninsula is divided. North Korea is a poor country, known to the outside world for its huge military parades. The wealthy cities of South Korea are famous for high-tech electronics.

HERDING GOATS, MONGOLIA

Taklimakan Desert

Tibetan Plateau

THE IMPERIAL PALACE ("FORBIDDEN CITY"), BEIJING

SHANGHAI
Shanghai is the world's leading seaport and China's biggest city, with a population of more than 24 million.

CHINESE DRAGON DANCE

ULAN BATOR ●

MONGOLIA

Gobi Desert

Hokkaido

NORTH
KOREA

SEA OF
JAPAN

BEIJING ●

PYONGYANG ●

CHINA

SEOUL ●
SOUTH
KOREA

JAPAN

TOKYO ●

Yellow R.

Yangtze R.

SHANGHAI ●

BRIGHT CITY LIGHTS, TOKYO

GUANGZHOU ●
MACAU ●
HONG KONG ●

SOUTH
CHINA
SEA

YAKS, TIBETAN PLATEAU

THE BIG AND THE SMALL

China has the top population stats, with more than **1.4 billion** citizens
• About **20 percent** of the world's population is Chinese
• **24 million** live in the city of Shanghai • Just since 1979, Shenzhen, China, has grown from a small village to a city of **3.5 million**
• That's more than in all of Mongolia, where there are only **2.9 million** people. It is the world's **least** crowded nation.

A LAND OF CONTRASTS

Japan's big-city lights, high-speed "bullet" trains, and automobile plants exist side by side with peaceful countryside, ancient temples, and traditions. Its islands lie on the Pacific Rim and are at risk from earthquakes and tsunamis. The land is mountainous, with farms and large cities on the coastal plains.

?

WHO OR WHAT AM I?

I have two black eyes, and my favorite snack is bamboo shoots.

ANSWER: A giant panda

WHO LIVES HERE?

The **Han** make up more than 90 percent of China's population, speaking various forms of the Chinese language. There are 55 other peoples recognized within China's borders, including the **Zhuang, Manchus, Hui, Uygur, Miao, Yi,** and **Tibetans**. In the wider region are the **Japanese, Koreans,** and **Mongolians**. The religious beliefs of the Far East include Daoism, Confucianism, and various forms of Buddhism, Shinto (in Japan), Islam, and Christianity.

Chanoyu is an **ancient Japanese ceremony** for preparing and serving **tea.**

FLYING THE FISH

Colorful paper carp and streamers called *koinobori* fly in the breeze to celebrate Japanese Children's Day on May 5. Why this fish? The carp is much admired because it uses all its strength and skills to swim upstream and leap up waterfalls. Special rice cakes filled with red bean paste, called *kashiwamochi*, are served as a treat on this day.

China is the world's third-largest country: **3,855,100 sq. mi.** (9,984,670 km²)—that's slightly bigger than the U.S.

The Great Wall is a vast series of defenses built across northern China over 1,000 years following the 600s B.C. All of its parts added together total **13,171 mi. (21,196 km).**

THE EASTERN ASIA REAL DEAL!

THE FORBIDDEN CITY:
The 600-year-old imperial palace in Beijng, with 980 buildings inside its walls

SHANGHAI TRANSRAPID:
This magnetic levitation train makes no contact with the track as it streaks along at 268 mph (431 km/h)

HOT AND COLD:
Temperatures in the Gobi Desert can vary by 63°F (35°C) in a single day

BLACK BELT:
Judo is Japan's leading martial art

SPRING FLOWERS AND PICNICS:
Hanami means cherry blossom time in Japan

FEARSOME FUGU:
Fugu raw fish is a big treat in Japan, but eat the right parts—some of it contains a deadly poison!

IN A PICKLE:
Kimchi (sour and spicy vegetables), the taste of Korea

SPORTS IN MONGOLIA:
Traditional archery, wrestling, and horse racing

Ancient Chinese inventions

- Fireworks • Acupuncture
- Cast iron • Lacquer
- Magnetic compass
- High-quality porcelain
- Nail polish
- Gunpowder
- Paper money
- Printing
- Chopsticks
- Kites
- Rudders for ships
- Seismometers
  (to record earthquakes)

The **Yangtze River,** or Chang Jiang, is **Asia's longest river** and the world's third longest, at **3,915 mi.** (6,300 km).

The **Yellow River** is Asia's second-longest river, and it got its name because it is so muddy. It is also known as **"China's Sorrow"** because of its devastating floods over the ages.

Japan is made up of 6,852 islands! Most people live on the four biggest ones—Honshu, Hokkaido, Kyushu, and Shikoku.

South Korea has the world's fastest broadband speed, with an average download throughput of

33.5 megabits per second

Poached, fried, or fossilized? **Dinosaur eggs** were discovered at the Flaming Cliffs site in **Mongolia**—as well as the fossils of sickle-clawed dinosaurs called velociraptors.

In 2013 **Japan** produced **7.9 million** cars

Southern Asia

Bangladesh – Bhutan – India – Maldives – Nepal – Pakistan – Sri Lanka

About 1.3 billion people live in India, the giant of Southern Asia. Its noisy city streets and train stations swarm with crowds. Markets sell mangoes and fiery spices. Ancient Hindu temples overlook hot, dusty fields waiting for the monsoon rains. Women in brightly colored saris wash clothes. Many Indians are poor, but India also has new high-tech industries and is changing fast.

India points southward into the Indian Ocean, with the island nation of Sri Lanka just across the Palk Strait. To the northwest are the cities of Pakistan and the broad valley of the Indus River. Many big rivers are fed by the snowy peaks of the Karakorum range. The gigantic Himalayas run eastward through Nepal and Bhutan along the Chinese border.

The Ganges River flows from the western Himalayas across the Indian plain, and in Bangladesh it spills into a maze of waterways. The low coast of the Bay of Bengal is fertile but often suffers from massive flooding.

THE GANGES AT VARANASI, SACRED TO HINDUS

A MAJESTIC MAUSOLEUM
The Taj Mahal in Agra, India, was built in 1653. Is this marble tomb the world's most beautiful building?

PICKING TEA IN SRI LANKA

Kashmir

Karakoram Mts.

ISLAMABAD

LAHORE

PAKISTAN

Punjab

Indus R.

KARACHI

NEW DELHI

Himalayan Mts.

NEPAL

KATHMANDU   Himalayan Mts.

Ganges R.

THIMPHU   BHUTAN

SIKH GOLDEN TEMPLE, AMRITSAR

BANGLADESH

DHAKA

INDIA

KOLKATA

K2—ON THE CHINA–PAKISTAN BORDER

MUMBAI   Deccan Plateau

BAY OF BENGAL

BANGALORE   CHENNAI

SOUTH TO THE ISLANDS
The Maldives are a group of coral islands in the Indian Ocean. They form the smallest country in Asia by area (115 sq. mi., or 298 km²) and by population (393,500). They are also the lowest lying, on average just 4 ft. 11 in. (1.5 m) above sea level.

SRI LANKA

COLOMBO

SUPER STATS
The Himalayas have more than 100 peaks higher than **23,600 ft.** (7,200 m) • Mt. Everest (Sagamartha or Chomolongma) is **29,029 ft.** (8,848 m) above sea level, and climbers can reach it from Nepal or from Tibet • The Ganges River travels **1,569 mi.** (2,525 km) from the Himalayas to the sea, where it forms the world's **biggest delta,** covering **41,000 sq. mi.** (105,000 km²).

WHO LIVES HERE?

The fact that 447 different languages are spoken in India, 72 in Pakistan, 41 in Bangladesh, and 25 in Bhutan tells you that Southern Asia is a region of many different peoples, customs, and beliefs. There are great differences between city dwellers and villagers, and in India among traditional social classes called castes. Religion plays an important part in many people's lives, whether they are **Hindus, Muslims, Sikhs, Jains, Parsis, Buddhists,** or **Christians**.

Legend has it that **Shah Jahan** (the Mughal leader responsible for building the **Taj Mahal**) had the hands of architects and workers chopped off once it was completed. This was to ensure that they never built anything like this again.

KINGDOM OF THE CLOUDS

The secretive Himalayan kingdom of Bhutan nestles between China and India. Tourists weren't allowed here until 1974, and the kingdom has kept its traditional dress, its masked dances, its archery competitions, and its architecture. Wildlife includes the takin (which looks like a cross between a cow and a goat), the golden langur monkey, and the clouded leopard.

India is the **largest country** in Southern Asia: **1,269,219 sq. mi.** (3,287,263 km²)

Battle of the colors! At the Hindu **spring festival of Holi**, people hurl brightly colored powder or dyes at each other in the street.

The bustling city of Karachi, Pakistan, is home to about **23.5 million** people.

Fire dancers, drummers, and illuminated elephants are all part of **Esala Perahera** (the Festival of the Tooth), a spectacular Buddhist festival in **Kandy, Sri Lanka.**

HAVEN FOR BENGAL TIGERS:
The Sundarbans region of Bangladesh and India

KULFI ICE CREAM:
Flavored with cardamom, mango, or pistachio, this treat is popular across the region

CRICKET:
Favorite sport in Pakistan, India, and Sri Lanka

BHUTAN'S NAME:
Means "land of the thunder dragon"

BASANT:
Pakistan's spring festival is marked by the flying of kites

INDIA-NET:
India has more than 205 million Internet users

TWIN TRIANGLE:
Nepal's sun-and-moon national flag has a unique shape

BOLLYWOOD BONANZA:
Mumbai is home of the supersuccessful Indian movie industry

About **4,600** years ago the **Indus valley region** already had fine cities such as Harappa and Mohenjo-Daro, with drainage, grain storage, street grids, and docks.

The world's oldest locomotive still in service is the **Fairy Queen**, built for the British East India Company in 1855. It hauls a tourist train—top speed **25 mph** (40 km/h).

India is known for its farming, fishing, and textiles, its call centers, and its IT companies.

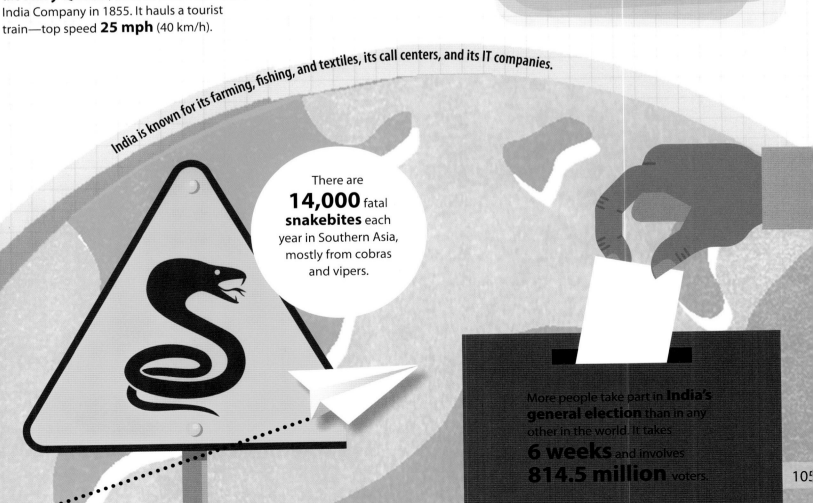

There are **14,000** fatal **snakebites** each year in Southern Asia, mostly from cobras and vipers.

More people take part in **India's general election** than in any other in the world. It takes **6 weeks** and involves **814.5 million** voters.

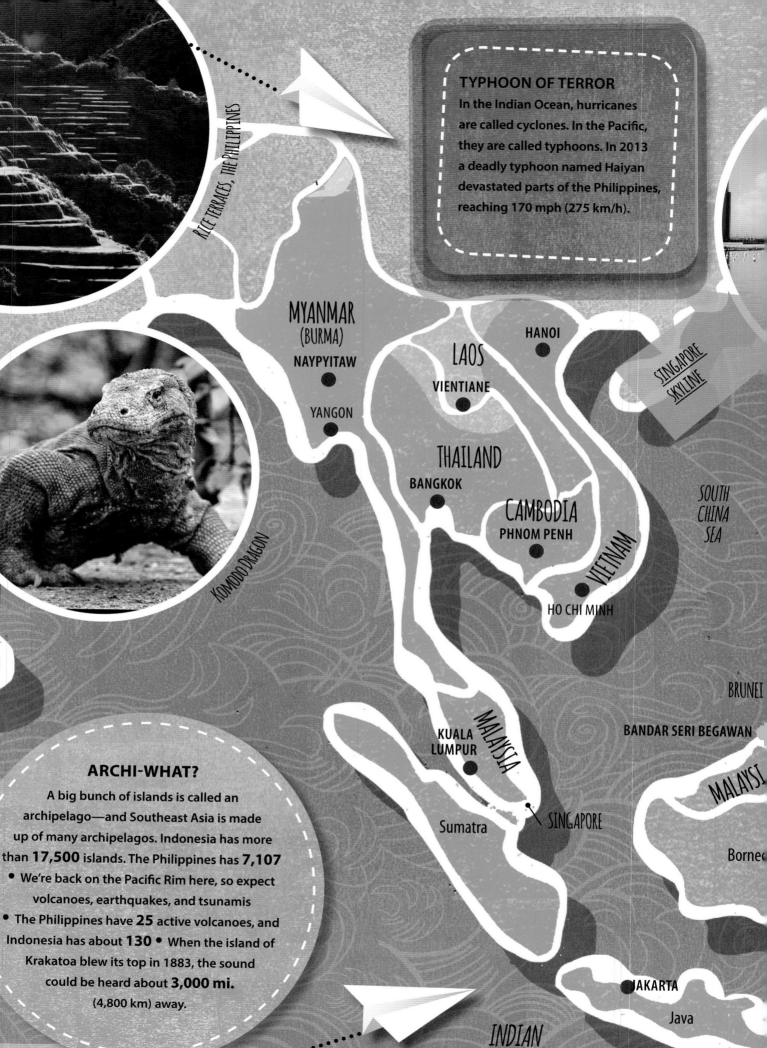

RICE TERRACES, THE PHILIPPINES

TYPHOON OF TERROR
In the Indian Ocean, hurricanes are called cyclones. In the Pacific, they are called typhoons. In 2013 a deadly typhoon named Haiyan devastated parts of the Philippines, reaching 170 mph (275 km/h).

MYANMAR
(BURMA)
NAYPYITAW

YANGON

LAOS

HANOI

VIENTIANE

SINGAPORE SKYLINE

THAILAND

BANGKOK

CAMBODIA

PHNOM PENH

VIETNAM

HO CHI MINH

SOUTH CHINA SEA

KOMODO DRAGON

BRUNEI

BANDAR SERI BEGAWAN

KUALA LUMPUR

MALAYSIA

MALAYSI

SINGAPORE

Sumatra

Borneo

ARCHI-WHAT?
A big bunch of islands is called an archipelago—and Southeast Asia is made up of many archipelagos. Indonesia has more than **17,500** islands. The Philippines has **7,107**
• We're back on the Pacific Rim here, so expect volcanoes, earthquakes, and tsunamis
• The Philippines have **25** active volcanoes, and Indonesia has about **130** • When the island of Krakatoa blew its top in 1883, the sound could be heard about **3,000 mi.** (4,800 km) away.

JAKARTA

Java

INDIAN OCEAN

Southeast Asia

BRUNEI - CAMBODIA - INDONESIA - LAOS - MALAYSIA - MYANMAR (BURMA)
PHILIPPINES - SINGAPORE - THAILAND - TIMOR-LESTE - VIETNAM

Between the Indian and Pacific oceans, the Asian continent forms a long peninsula. Large and small islands enclose warm seas, where flying fishes skim the waves. Laos, Vietnam, and Cambodia are lands of forests and flooded rice paddies, crossed by the Mekong River.

In the west, bordered by both India and China, Myanmar surrounds another great river, the Irrawaddy. A neck of land extends southward through Thailand, with its tropical beaches and islands, to Malaysia and Singapore. Both Singapore and Kuala Lumpur are hubs of international business.

Part of the island of Borneo also belongs to Malaysia, and part to the small country of Brunei. The rest of Borneo's tropical forests and mountains are in Indonesia, which also includes Java and Sumatra, as well as the western region of the island of New Guinea. Timor-Leste is an independent state in the south.

Between the South China Sea and the open Pacific are the Philippines, a maze of islands with forests, ancient rice terraces, and crowded cities. Manila, the capital, is on the island of Luzon.

Luzon

MANILA

PHILIPPINES

Mindanao

PHILIPPINE SEA

North
Maluku

INDONESIA

Maluku

Sulawesi

New Guinea

DILI
TIMOR-LESTE

WHO LIVES HERE?

Peoples of Southeast Asia include the **Thais, Tai, Annamese, Khmer, Lao, Malays, Dayaks, ethnic Chinese, Javanese, Filipino,** and hundreds of other ethnic groups. In Indonesia alone 706 languages can be heard, and in the Philippines 181. Many religions are found here—Roman Catholic Christianity in the Philippines, Buddhism from Thailand to Vietnam, and Hinduism on the island of Bali. Indonesia has the world's biggest Muslim population, of about 205 million.

There are about **3 million** water buffalo in Vietnam, more than **3 million** in the Philippines, and **1.3 million** in Thailand. Despite their big horns, they are friendly creatures used for plowing rice fields.

BOY MONKS OF MYANMAR

The boy monks from Myanmar (Burma) wear the simple robes of a Buddhist monk and carry a bowl for offerings. Most males in the country shave their heads and join a monastery as a trainee monk between the ages of 10 and 20, and again as a full monk when they are an adult. They may lead the life of a monk for just a few days—or for a lifetime.

Indonesia is the largest country in Southeast Asia: **735,358 sq. mi.** (1,904,569 km²)

Angkor Wat in Cambodia is the biggest religious monument in the world. It was built by the Khmer people in the 1100s as a Hindu temple and later became a center of Buddhism.

THE NAME SINGAPORE:
Means "lion city"

SPICE ISLANDS:
Indonesia produces the most cloves of anywhere—about 57,000 tons a year

TALL TOWERS:
Petronas Towers, twin skyscrapers, Kuala Lumpur (1,483 ft., or 452 m)

PINEAPPLE CHUNKS:
The Philippines is the biggest pineapple producer in the world

ORANGUTAN:
Meet the hairiest of the great apes, in Borneo or Sumatra

MUAY THAI BOXING:
Combat sport using feet, knees, and elbows, as well as fists

PHO BO:
Beef noodle soup, delicious street food from Vietnam

PEACH BLOSSOM:
Is used to celebrate Tet, the Vietnamese New Year

FABULOUS FABRICS:
Batik patterned textiles from Java

Greater Jakarta is the most populous city area in Southeast Asia. It is home to more than **28 million** Indonesians.

Thailand's top exports are computers and computer accessories, while Indonesia's are oil, gas, and palm oil.

Indonesia's precious **tropical forests** are being destroyed by **illegal logging**. The burning of forest for farming often chokes the cities with smog.

The world's **biggest lizard** is the **Komodo dragon** of Indonesia.

It can grow up to **10 ft.** (3 m) long and weigh **150 lb.** (70 kg).

DO YOU WANT TO GO TO . . .

KrungthepmahanakhonAmonrattanakosinMahintharayutthaya MahadilokphopNoppharatratchathaniburiromUdomratchaniwet mahasathanAmonphimanawatansathitSakkathattiyawitsanukamprasit
. . . THIS WAY

AT THE AIRPORT THEY JUST CALL IT . . . BANGKOK!

The **Shwedagon pagoda** in **Yangon**, Myanmar (Burma), is covered in gold. Its crown is set with **5,448 diamonds** and **2,317 rubies.** The tip is topped with a **76-carat diamond.**

Southwest Asia

Bahrain - Cyprus - Iran - Iraq - Israel & the Palestinian territories - Jordan - Kuwait
Lebanon - Oman - Qatar - Saudi Arabia - Syria - Turkey - United Arab Emirates (UAE) - Yemen

Iranian herders lead their sheep and goats into the mountains through melting snows. Construction workers put the finishing touches on a gleaming new skyscraper, high above Dubai. An Iraqi man harvests the season's dates. This region, often called the Middle East, is where humans first farmed and built the first cities. Many empires and civilizations arose here over the ages. In our own times these lands have suffered from war and violence. Oil and gas have brought great wealth to some countries, but many people remain poor.

Iran lies between the Caspian Sea and the shimmering heat haze of the Persian Gulf. Iraq occupies the valleys of the Tigris and Euphrates rivers. To the south are the small but wealthy Gulf states, and also Yemen, Oman, and the deserts of Saudi Arabia. The sandy wilderness runs on into Jordan. Syria, Lebanon, and Israel all have coasts on the eastern Mediterranean, while the Palestinian territories include Gaza and the West Bank. The historic city of Jerusalem is revered by Jews, Muslims, and Christians alike.

North of the island of Cyprus, Turkey forms a great bridge between Asia and Europe, and its largest city, Istanbul, stands on the divide. Many Turkish villagers are leaving the countryside, with its olive groves, rolling grasslands, and mountains, to work in the growing cities.

ORANGE ORCHARD, CYPRUS

ISTANBUL

IZMIR

JERUSALEM, HOLY CITY

SAND DUNES, UNITED ARAB EMIRATES

THE BLUE MOSQUE IN ISTANBUL OVERLOOKS THE BOSPORUS TO ASIA

BLACK SEA

CASPIAN SEA

OIL WELL, MARMUL, DHOFAR, OMAN

● ANKARA

TURKEY

SYRIA

CYPRUS

LEBANON
● **BEIRUT**
● **DAMASCUS**

● JERUSALEM ● **AMMAN**

JORDAN

ISRAEL & THE
PALESTINIAN
TERRITORIES

● MOSUL

IRAQ

● **BAGHDAD**

● BASRA

KUWAIT

● **KUWAIT
CITY**

● TEHRAN

IRAN

● MASHHAD

● ISFAHAN

Dasht-e Lut Desert

SAUDI ARABIA

● **RIYADH**

PERSIAN GULF

● MANAMA

BAHRAIN

QATAR ● ● **DOHA**

● **DUBAI**

**UNITED
ARAB EMIRATES**

● **MUSCAT**

Arabian Desert

RED SEA

OMAN

YEMEN

● SANA'A

● ADEN

PERSIAN LEOPARD

SAND AND SALT

Fly over the Arabian Desert and it just seems to go on and on—and on . . . It has an area of about **899,618 sq. mi.** (2,330,000 km²) ● At its heart is a great wilderness of sand called Rub'al-Khali, the Empty Quarter ● The longest rivers of the Middle East are the Tigris (**1,180 mi.,** or 1,899 km) and the Euphrates (**2,235 mi.,** or 3,596 km) ● The salty waters of the Dead Sea lie between Jordan, the Palestinian West Bank, and Israel. This is the lowest point on the planet, at **1,401 ft.** (427 m) below sea level.

ANCIENT CIVILIZATIONS
ASSYRIAN CARVING,
800s B.C.

Saudi Arabia is the biggest country in the area: **83,0000 sq. mi.** (2,149,690 km²)

Over **3 million** Muslim pilgrims may attend the annual **Hajj** in **Mecca, Saudi Arabia**. It is the holiest city of Islam.

WHO LIVES HERE?

The most widespread people of Southwest Asia are the **Arabs**. Other major groups include the **Iranians**, the **Turks** and the **Jews**. The **Kurdish** people live in Turkey, Iran, Iraq and Syria. Both **Turks** and **Greeks** live on Cyprus. There are many other minority peoples, languages and cultures. Islam is the faith with the most followers in the region. It includes Muslims of both the Sunni and the Shi'a branches. Judaism is the religion of Jews in Israel and elsewhere. There are several local Christian churches and traditions.

FLEEING THE WAR

Can you imagine having to leave your home at a moment's notice? You have no time to grab your favourite things. War broke out in Syria in 2011, between rebels and the government. It was terrible living in the cities as bombs were falling. Many people fled across the borders to other countries, to escape the terror. They had to live in tents. By 2014, 589,000 Syrians were living in Jordan. Another 992,000 were in Lebanon and 668,000 in Turkey. It might be years before they can go home again.

Ancient Inventions of the Middle East

- c. 9500 B.C. **Farming**
- c. 4000 B.C. **Towns**
- c. 3500 B.C. **Wheeled vehicles, the potter's wheel, writing, bronze**
- c. 2350 B.C. **Libraries**
- 2334 **The first empire (Akkad)**

Call it the original shopping mall. **Istanbul's Grand Bazaar** was founded in **1456,** and it can still attract up to 400,000 visitors each day. It has 61 covered streets with more than 3,000 stores.

The sunshine island of **Cyprus** is a big grower of citrus fruits—**grapefruit, oranges, and lemons.**

SHADOW PUPPETS:
An ancient Turkish tradition

HIDDEN CITY OF PETRA:
Ancient desert city carved from pink sandstone, Jordan

PALESTINIAN SWEET:
Maamoul—dates or walnuts dipped in sweet semolina

MUDHIF:
Beautiful reed architecture in the marshes of southern Iraq

"HELLO" IN KURDISH:
Pronounced "silaw"

NOWRUZ:
Iran's ancient spring festival

SPOTTED—BUT SELDOM SPOTTED!:
The rare Persian leopard of northern Iran and eastern Turkey

BIG SAUDI SPORT:
Camel racing (top speed 40 mph, or 65 km/h)

Saudi Arabia has almost one-fifth of the world's proven oil reserves and is the largest producer and exporter of oil in the world.

159.3°F
(70.7°C)

The **hottest** surface temperatures on Earth have been recorded by satellite and located in the Dasht-e Lut salt desert of **eastern Iran**.

Pumping fuel . . . **5 of the world's top 10 oil producers** are from the Middle East—**Saudi Arabia, Iran, Iraq, United Arab Emirates, Kuwait.**

Africa

> "I dream of an Africa which is at peace with itself."
>
> Nelson Mandela (1918–2013)

Africa is a land of big skies and fiery sunsets. Here you can see some of the last great herds of wild animals on our planet. Ancient fossils in the rocks show that this is where human beings first evolved and where we all have our roots.

Today Africa has more young people under the age of 20 than any other continent. That means hope. You can feel the buzz and energy in school classrooms, on the busy streets of the big cities, in distant villages.

Hundreds of years ago there were great African kingdoms and empires, but most of the continents came under the control of other countries. Some Africans were sold into slavery. Today most African countries rule themselves, but many still face problems, such as poor health and lack of clean water. Droughts make life hard on farmers. Many people have been troubled by war, crime, and poverty. Young Africans want another kind of future.

MADEIRA ISLANDS (PORTUGAL)

CANARY ISLANDS (SPAIN)

MOROCCO

Atlas Mts

WESTERN SAHARA

MAURITANIA

CAPE VERDE

Niger R.

BURKINA FA

SENEGAL

THE GAMBIA

GUINEA-BISSAU

GUINEA

SIERRA LEONE

LIBERIA

CÔTE D'IVORE

GHANA

EQUATOR

ASCENSION ISLAND

ATLANTIC OCEAN

12

Most of Africa is divided into four time zones, running north to south. Two more time zones cover the Cape Verde islands in the far west and Mauritius and the Seychelles far to the east.

MAP KEY
1 Kora harp 2 The Great Mosque, Djenné 3 Galago (bush baby) 4 Ancient Egyptian statue of a cat 5 Baobab tree 6 Mountain gorilla 7 Cocoa bean 8 Okapi 9 Red-hot poker flower 10 Ndebele painted house 11 Elephant 12 Leatherback turtle 13 Southern right whale dolphin 14 Container ship

Area: 11,668,598 sq. mi. (30,221,532 km²)
Fact: second-largest continent
Population: 1.1 billion

ASIA

TUNISIA

MEDITERRANEAN SEA

ALGERIA

ara Desert

LIBYA

EGYPT

4

LI

BENIN

NIGER

CHAD

SUDAN

Nile R.

RED SEA

ERITREA

DJIBOUTI

ETHIOPIA

NIGERIA

3

Blue Nile

SOMALILAND

EQUATORIAL
GUINEA

CAMEROON

CENTRAL
AFRICAN REPUBLIC

5

White Nile

SOUTH SUDAN

TOGO

BIOKO
ISLAND

Congo R.

GABON

CONGO

UGANDA

RWANDA

6

KENYA

SOMALIA

14

EQUATOR

SÃO TOMÉ
& PRINCIPE

DEMO.
REP. OF
CONGO

8

BURUNDI

11

TANZANIA

SEYCHELLES

Lualaba R.

MALAWI

COMOROS

MAYOTTE
(FRANCE)

ANGOLA

ZAMBIA

Zambezi R.

MOZAMBIQUE

MADAGASCAR

REUNION
(FRANCE)

ZIMBABWE

13

Namib Desert

NAMIBIA

BOTSWANA

SOUTH AFRICA

SWAZILAND

MAURITIUS

9

LESOTHO

10

INDIAN
OCEAN

Amazing Africa

In Kenya there is a line painted across the road marking the equator. You can place one foot on each side so that you are standing on the northern and southern halves of the globe. The equator runs right across the middle of Africa. Much of the region is warm and steamy. Its rain forests support chimpanzees, gorillas, okapi, and more than 11,000 plant species. Heavy rains fill the lakes and big rivers, the home of crocodiles and hippos. To the north and south there are dry grasslands, known as savanna, where the lion is king. There are great deserts and mountains, too. The highest mountains have snowy peaks, even in hot countries.

The Nile is the world's longest river, at **4,285 mi.** (6,853 km)

ZAMBEZI RIVER, ZAMBIA

LIBYAN DESERT

MOUNT KILIMANJARO, TANZANIA

Magnificent African animals

The African elephant is the world's biggest land mammal • A bull elephant can weigh over **6 tons** • The gangly giraffe is a walking skyscraper, standing about **20 ft. (6 m)** tall • The ostrich is the biggest bird in the world and the fastest on land, at about **43 mph (70 km/h)** • All of these animals live within sight of Africa's highest mountain, Kilimanjaro, which rises to **19,340 ft. (5,895 m)**.

GREAT WHITE PELICANS, SOUTHERN AFRICA

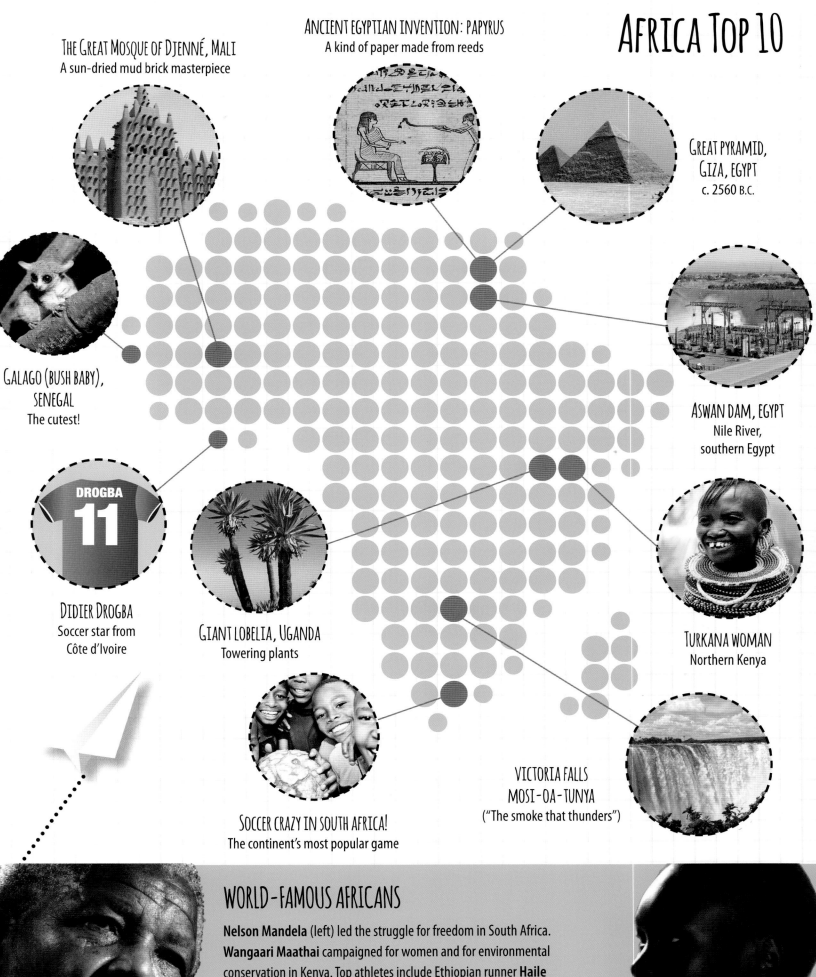

AFRICA TOP 10

THE GREAT MOSQUE OF DJENNÉ, MALI
A sun-dried mud brick masterpiece

ANCIENT EGYPTIAN INVENTION: PAPYRUS
A kind of paper made from reeds

GREAT PYRAMID, GIZA, EGYPT
c. 2560 B.C.

GALAGO (BUSH BABY), SENEGAL
The cutest!

ASWAN DAM, EGYPT
Nile River, southern Egypt

DROGBA 11

DIDIER DROGBA
Soccer star from Côte d'Ivoire

GIANT LOBELIA, UGANDA
Towering plants

TURKANA WOMAN
Northern Kenya

SOCCER CRAZY IN SOUTH AFRICA!
The continent's most popular game

VICTORIA FALLS MOSI-OA-TUNYA
("The smoke that thunders")

WORLD-FAMOUS AFRICANS

Nelson Mandela (left) led the struggle for freedom in South Africa. **Wangaari Maathai** campaigned for women and for environmental conservation in Kenya. Top athletes include Ethiopian runner **Haile Gebrselassie** (b. 1973). **Alek Wek** (right), born in South Sudan in 1977, is a supermodel, and a galaxy of African musicians are international stars.

Northern Africa

Algeria - Chad - Egypt - Libya - Mali - Mauritania -
Morocco - Niger - Sudan - Tunisia - Western Sahara

There is an amazing square called Djemaa el-Fna in
Marrakesh, Morocco. Join the crowds and you can smell
delicious spices and see dancers, storytellers, snake
charmers, and water sellers in traditional clothes.
In North Africa you will also see farmers picking olives by the
Mediterranean Sea, or modern city streets and busy college
students and office workers in Internet cafés. To the south are
the mountain ranges of the Atlas and the vast wilderness of
the Sahara Desert. In the south the Sahara fringes the
Sahel region, often dry but grazed by goats and cattle.
Eastward, the Nile surges through the deserts of
Sudan and Egypt, providing life—water for
humans, animals, and crops, as well as
hydropower for cities.

SPICE MARKET, MARRAKESH, MOROCCO

MADEIRA ISLANDS
(PORTUGAL)

CANARY ISLANDS
(SPAIN)

WESTERN SAHARA

MAURITANIA

● NOUAKCHOTT

CAPE VERDE

BAMAKO
●

AN ERG VIPER FROM THE SAHARA

DESERTED DESERT
Few people cross the rocks and sand
dunes of the Sahara other than oil and gas
workers and traders with their camels.

CAMELS CROSSING!!

RABAT
MOROCCO
Atlas Mts.

ALGIERS

TUNIS

TUNISIA

TRIPOLI

MEDITERRANEAN SEA

Suez Canal

ASIA

Sinai

CAIRO

Sahara Desert

ALGERIA

LIBYA

Libyan esert

EGYPT

Lake Nasser

Ahaggar Mts.

Tibesti Mts.

RED SEA

MALI

Niger R.

NIGER

CHAD

SUDAN

Nile R.

NIAMEY

Sahel

Lake Chad

N'DJAMENA

KHARTOUM

Blue Nile

MANY HOUSES ARE FLAT ROOFED AND DESIGNED TO KEEP COOL IN THE FIERCE HEAT.

AFRICAN PATTERN

PRECIOUS WATER

In some parts of the desert there is water trapped deep underground in rocks. At oases this water is brought to the surface through channels and wells. Plants can grow here and provide shade. Dates can be harvested. Goats or camels can be brought to the oases for water.

SUPER STATS

More than **9 million** people live in Cairo, the biggest city in North Africa ● The pyramids of Giza were built over **4,500 years** ago as tombs for Egyptian kings, or pharaohs ● The Blue Nile and the White Nile join up in Sudan and flow northward to the Mediterranean, forming a great delta. The Nile River pumps out **99,940 cu. ft. (2,830 m³)** of water every second (that's almost 19,000 full bathtubs!).

?

WHO OR WHAT AM I?

I have eight legs, two big pincers, and a nasty stinger in my tail.

ANSWER: A scorpion

WHO LIVES HERE?

Peoples of North Africa include **Arabs** and various groups of **Berbers**, such as the Tuareg. South of the Sahara are black African peoples such as the **Fulani.** Most North Africans are **Muslims.** In Egypt there are also **Christians** of the Coptic Church.

The **Dogon** population today is around 300,000. Many live in small villages, around 700 of them with populations of less than 500. These villages are made up of caves that are carved into the **124 mi.–long** (200 km–long) Bandiagara cliffs in Mali.

GOBBLING GOATS

Spring comes early to the Rif Mountains in northern Morocco. Families grow figs and corn, and many raise cattle or goats. There is plenty of green grass for the animals to eat. The trouble is that the goats strip almost every plant in sight. Herders have to keep them out of the precious forests of cedar, which grow high on the slopes.

Algeria is the largest country in all of Africa at **919,595 sq. mi.** (2,381,741 km²)

The Dogon people of Mali perfom dances and ceremonies on stilts.

Locusts are hungry grasshopppers that destroy crops when they swarm. There may be **129 million** of them in just **1 sq. mi.** (2.6 km²). That's **42 per sq. yd.!**

Egyptians own the most cell phones in North Africa— **92,640,000.**

After a long journey in the desert, a camel can gulp down **36 gal. (135 L)** of water in just **13 minutes!**

In dry lands, rainfall is a matter of **life or death.**

Egypt produces **1,515,000 tons** (1,374,000 metric tons) of dates every year—and that's a world record!

"HELLO" IN TUNISIA:
As-salam alaykum

HIGHEST MOUNTAIN:
Toubkal, Morocco: 13,671 ft. (4,167 m)

DEADLIEST SCORPION IN THE SAHARA:
The deathstalker

WORLD'S OLDEST UNIVERSITY:
Al-karouine, Fès, Morocco
(founded A.D. 859)

EGYPT'S FAVORITE BOARD GAME :
Backgammon

AMAZING ROMAN RUINS:
Leptis Magna, Libya c. A.D. 200

FABULOUS FOOD:
Steamed couscous

SMELLIEST PLACE:
Leather works, Fès, Morocco
(hides are soaked in pigeon poop)

ANCIENT EGYPTIAN CUSTOM:
Mummified crocodiles

Morocco and Western Sahara contain three-fourths of all the world's phosphates, which are used in making fertilizers for crops.

Temperatures in the Sahara Desert can soar above **122°F (50°C).**

122⁰

Trains in Mauritania can be up to 1.6 mi. (2.5 km) long, with more than 200 wagons carrying iron ore through the desert.

Eastern Africa

BURUNDI – COMOROS – DJIBOUTI – ETHIOPIA – ERITREA – KENYA – MAYOTTE
RWANDA – SEYCHELLES – SOMALIA – SOUTH SUDAN – TANZANIA – UGANDA

Journeys can take you to all types of places—coffee farms, forests, cities, or villages of thatched huts. Why not take a bus? You may be sharing it with chickens going to market . . . or maybe ride on a train or a truck or a crazily crowded matatu minibus. That can be a bumpy ride, but you're sure to meet all kinds of people and hear many different languages. Inland are the deserts of Somalia, the highlands of Ethiopia, the Blue Nile and White Nile rivers, and the Great Rift Valley. To the west are Africa's Great Lakes and the green hills and red earth of Uganda, Rwanda, and Burundi.

GREAT RIFT VALLEY, TANZANIA

ON SAFARI, KENYA

BUSTLING LOCAL MARKET, BURUNDI

BENEATH THE HIGHEST PEAK
Elephants roam the dusty savanna beneath the snowy slopes of Kilimanjaro, Africa's highest mountain.

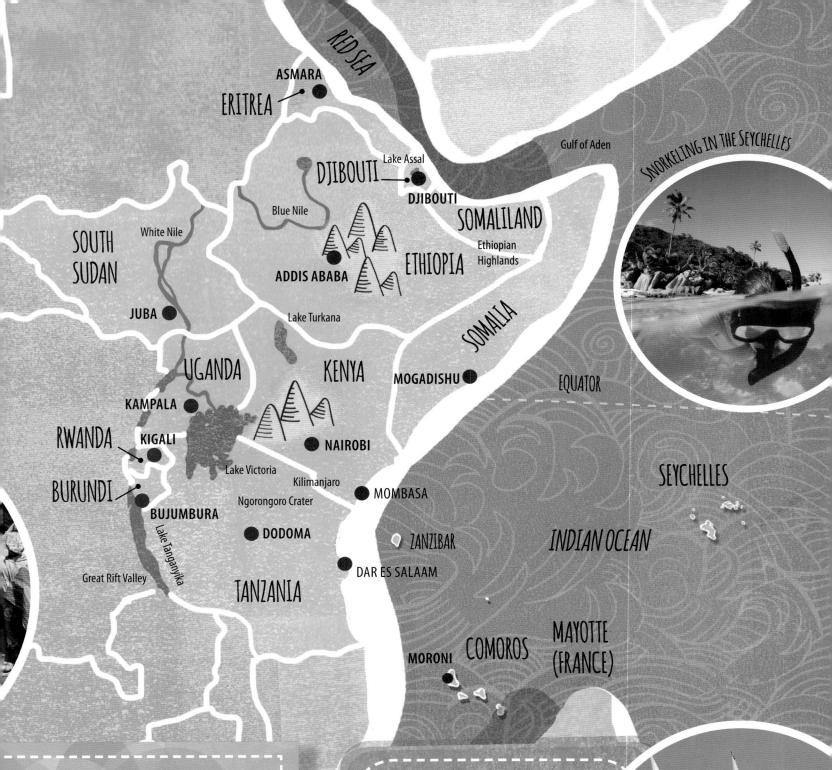

RED SEA

ASMARA

ERITREA

DJIBOUTI

Lake Assal

DJIBOUTI

Gulf of Aden

SNORKELING IN THE SEYCHELLES

SOUTH SUDAN

White Nile

Blue Nile

ADDIS ABABA

ETHIOPIA

Ethiopian Highlands

SOMALILAND

JUBA

Lake Turkana

SOMALIA

UGANDA

KENYA

MOGADISHU

EQUATOR

KAMPALA

NAIROBI

RWANDA

KIGALI

Lake Victoria

SEYCHELLES

BURUNDI

Kilimanjaro

BUJUMBURA

Ngorongoro Crater

MOMBASA

Lake Tanganyika

DODOMA

ZANZIBAR

INDIAN OCEAN

DAR ES SALAAM

Great Rift Valley

TANZANIA

MORONI

COMOROS

MAYOTTE (FRANCE)

NATURAL WONDERS

Lake Victoria is an inland sea, the biggest in Africa, with an area of **42,750 mi. (68,800 km)** • The lowest place in Africa is Lake Assal, in Djibouti, which lies **508 ft. (155 m) below sea level**. Its waters are 10 times saltier than the ocean • One awesome place to watch wildlife is in an extinct volcano—the **Ngorongoro crater** in Tanzania • **Footprints** found in the rocks there at Laetoli show that distant relatives of humans were walking on two feet **3.6 million years ago.**

INDIAN OCEAN SHIPPING

Small wooden dhows sail the coasts and islands, carrying mangrove timber, building materials, or fresh catches of fish. Big cargo ships and tankers head for ports such as Mombasa or Dar es Salaam.

?

WHO OR WHAT AM I?

I'm big and fat, with little ears and huge front teeth. I can swim underwater and get very angry.

ANSWER: A hippo

WHO LIVES HERE?

Hundreds of different peoples live in these regions. Meet the **Amhara** of Ethiopia; the **Nuer** and **Dinka** of South Sudan; the **Maasai** of Kenya and Tanzania; the **Baganda** of Uganda; the **Hutu** and **Tutsis** of Rwanda . . . There are also **Asian** and **European** communities. There are Christians, Muslims, and followers of traditional African beliefs.

Eritrea was the first country in the world to make its whole coastline of **837 mi.** (1,347 km) a protected conservation zone.

HOW DOES YOUR SCHOOL COMPARE?

In Kenya, the school year starts in January and there are three terms. From ages 6 to 14 you have to go to primary school, although in rural and poor areas many children don't attend. You will learn English and Swahili and math. If you pass your exams, you may go on to secondary school or other training.

The largest country in eastern Africa is **Ethiopia**, with a total area of **426,373 sq. mi.** (1,104,300 km²).

These children wear blue-and-orange uniforms to attend their school in Iloileri, near **Kenya's Amboseli National Park.**

More than **4 in every 10** Kenyans are under the **age of 14.**

THE EASTERN AFRICA REAL DEAL!

13

Ethiopia has **13 months**. Why? Because Ethiopia follows an ancient Christian calendar, which has an extra month of 5 or 6 days.

Flamingos get their pink color from tiny bacteria in the water that they swallow.

The island of Zanzibar exports cloves, nutmeg, black pepper, and cinnamon.

One Nile crocodile from Tanzania weighed about **2,400 lb. (1,090 kg)** and was almost **21 ft. (6.5 m)** long. That's the length of **two adult swimmers!**

21 ft. (6.5 m)

"HELLO" IN THE SWAHILI LANGUAGE:
Jambo!

FAVORITE BOARD GAME:
Bao (a version of mancala)

AMAZING BUILDINGS:
Rock-cut churches, Lalibela, Ethiopia

MAKING MUSIC:
The mbira (metal keys attached to a board)

GORILLA ID:
The nostils of every gorilla are unique, like a fingerprint.

POPULAR SNACK:
Mandazi doughnuts

DEEPEST LAKE:
Tanganyika— 4,820 ft. (1,470 m)

COFFEE ORIGINS:
The coffee bush may have originally come from Ethiopia.

Ethiopia is the fifth-biggest producer of coffee in the world.

Clean **water** from faucets is hard to come by in remote areas of **East Africa.** You may have to fetch water from a distant well instead of going into school.

Kenya has won **25 gold medals** at the Olympics, mostly for long-distance running.

25

Central & West Africa

BENIN – BURKINA FASO – CAMEROON – CAPE VERDE – CENTRAL AFRICAN REPUBLIC
CONGO – CÔTE D'IVOIRE – DEMOCRATIC REPUBLIC OF CONGO – EQUITORIAL GUINEA
GABON – THE GAMBIA – GHANA – GUINEA – GUINEA-BISSAU – LIBERIA – NIGERIA
SÃO TOMÉ & PRINCIPE – SENEGAL – SIERRA LEONE – TOGO

Welcome to the heart of Africa—a land of great forests and rivers. There are rich company-owned mines and oil wells in some regions, yet many people suffer from poverty and wars.

Long ago, peoples from around the Niger and Congo rivers spread out across the continent. Their wonderful masks and carvings have become classic images of Africa and are highly prized by collectors all over the world.

Central Africa is warm and humid, with thunder and heavy rains. These feed the waterways that flow into the Congo River on its long journey to the Atlantic Ocean. The huge forests of the Congo region extend into West Africa, but as you travel north, they give way to grasslands and then dry and dusty plains.

CLOUD FOREST
Moisture from the clouds ensures that green forests cover the mountain slopes of Central Africa.

CAPE VERDE

SENEGAL

DAKAR

BANJUL

THE GAMBIA

BISSAU

GUINEA-BISSAU

CONAKRY

FREETOWN

SIERRA LEONE

MONRO

RITUAL MASK, CAMEROON

YOUNG LOWLAND GORILLA, GABON

GUINEA

BURKINA FASO
● OUAGADOUGOU

CÔTE D'IVOIRE

GHANA
Lake Volta

TOGO

BENIN

Niger R.

NIGERIA
● ABUJA

BENUE

LAGOS

LIBERIA

ABIDJAN

ACCRA

LOMÉ

PORTO-NOVO

BIOKU ISLAND

SÃO TOMÉ
& PRINCIPE

EQUATOR

ATLANTIC
OCEAN

EQUATORIAL
GUINEA

LIBREVILLE

GABON

CAMEROON
● YAOUNDÉ

CENTRAL
AFRICAN REPUBLIC
● BANGUI

CONGO

Congo R.

DEMOCRATIC
REPUBLIC OF
CONGO

BRAZZAVILLE

KINSHASA

CABINDA
(ANGOLA)

Lualaba R.

THE CONGO BASIN

DEADLY LAKES
Three lakes in Central Africa are killers!
Lakes Nyos (right), Monoun, and Kivu fill
up with undergound volcanic gas.
The lakes may explode or leak
deadly gas into the air, killing
people who live nearby.

RIVERS AND RAIN
The Congo River is the longest river
in this region, at **2,900 mi.** (4,700 km).
In places it is also the world's deepest, at over
722 ft. (220 m). It gives its name to two
countries, the **Republic of Congo** on the
north bank and **D.R. Congo** (the Democratic
Republic) on the south ● By the way, don't
forget to take an umbrella to Debundscha, by
Mount Cameroon—it's the wettest place in all
of Africa, with rainfall of **400 in.**
(10,299 mm) a year.

?

WHO OR WHAT AM I?
I can change color, swivel my
eyes, and zap a fly with my long,
long tongue.

ANSWER: A chameleon

WHO LIVES HERE?

So many different peoples live in these regions—**Wolof, Fulani, Ewe, Fon, Akan, Igbo, Hausa, Yoruba, Kongo, Luba** . . . They may live in big cities or remote villages. They may be Christians, Muslims, or followers of traditional African beliefs such as Vodun. In the rain forests peoples such as the Baka and Mbuti still hunt and gather wild food.

The **Congo Rain Forest** is the second-largest on the planet and covers about **694,984 sq. mi.** (1,800,000 km²).

THE KINSUKA KIDS

White water marks the start of the Livingstone Falls, 217 mi. (350 km) of rocks and swirling currents. This water is WILD! The rapids sound like thunder. Kids come here to cool off in the foam when the weather gets too hot and sticky. They are from Kinsuka, not far from the big, noisy city of Kinshasa, in the Democratic Republic of Congo.

D.R. Congo is the largest country in the Central and West region, with a total area of **905,355 sq. mi.** (2,345,409 km²)

Sallah is a splendid **Islamic festival** held in Nigeria. Horseback riders in rich costume gallop by to honor the local ruler.

THE CENTRAL & WEST AFRICA REAL DEAL!

A saying from Senegal: **Sahha kënz ihahayaat.** Health is a treasure.

"HELLO" IN THE YORUBA LANGUAGE:
Kaabo

POPULAR SNACK:
African yam chips

BIGGEST ECONOMY IN AFRICA:
Nigeria, thanks to oil

TOP SOCCER COUNTRIES:
Nigeria, Ghana, Cameroon

SMALLEST COUNTRY IN MAINLAND AFRICA:
The Gambia (4,127 sq. mi., or 10,689 km²)

MEGA LAND SNAIL:
Ghana's giant African snail is the world's biggest

UNIQUE PLANTS:
3,300 species found only in the Congo Rain Forest

EYO FESTIVAL:
Costumed dancers and masquerades in Lagos, Nigeria

WEST AFRICA'S LONGEST:
Niger River (2,600 mi., or 4,180 km)

West Africa produces about **two-thirds** of all the world's **cocoa.**

2/3

Copper and cobalt from D.R. Congo are used in making **cell phones.** Some children as young as six or seven have to work in the mines.

D.R. Congo probably has about $24 trillion worth of minerals still to be mined. They include cobalt, diamonds, gold, copper, and tungsten.

The **Akan people of Ghana** often name their children after the day of the week on which they were born. The name "Kwasi," for example, comes from "Sunday."

In West Africa a **kola nut** is a gift to show friendship or hospitality.

Nigeria has the biggest movie industry in Africa, earning it the nickname **"Nollywood."**

The **Gaboon viper** has the longest fangs of any venomous snake, at **2 in. (5 cm).**

Southern Africa

Angola - Botswana - Lesotho - Madagascar - Malawi - Mauritius - Mozambique
Namibia - Réunion - South Africa - Swaziland - Zambia - Zimbabwe

A young man checks into work at the oil terminal at the port of Beira, Mozambique. In Angola a group of women dig potatoes, with their babies bundled on their backs. In a market in Malawi, women are selling bananas. Student nurses are caring for hospital patients in Lusaka, Zambia. It's another day in Southern Africa.

The continent of Africa narrows to the south, where the great slab of Table Mountain looks out over Cape Town and the open ocean. Southern Africa has tropical forests, grasslands, bush, and mountain ranges such as the Drakensbergs. Here are big rivers, such as the Zambezi, the Okavango, the Limpopo, and the Orange, but also the parched deserts of the Kalahari and the Namib.

SOUTHERN CITY
Cape Town, beside Table Bay in South Africa, is a city of 3.7 million people.

ATLANTIC OCEAN

LUANDA

ANGOLA

NAMIBIA

Namib Desert

WINDHOEK

Cape of Good Hope

CAPE TOWN

PICKING GRAPES IN THE WESTERN CAPE, SOUTH AFRICA

VICTORIA FALLS
(MOSI-OA-TUNYA) ON THE ZAMBIA-ZIMBABWE BORDER

MALAWI

Lake Malawi (Nyasa)

ZAMBIA

LUSAKA

LILONGWE

Zambezi R.

HARARE

MOZAMBIQUE

Victoria Falls

ZIMBABWE

BOTSWANA

MADAGASCAR

MAURITIUS

MOZAMBIQUE CHANNEL

ANTANANARIVO

PORT LOUIS

GABORONE

PRETORIA (TSHWANE)

Kalahari Desert

MAPUTO

RÉUNION (FRANCE)

JOHANNESBURG

MBABANE

SWAZILAND

INDIAN OCEAN

Orange R.

DURBAN

BLOEMFONTEIN

MASERU

SOUTH AFRICA

LESOTHO

ZEBRAS AT A WATER HOLE

BAOBAB TREES IN MADAGASCAR

WILD FACTS

Madagascar, which is **226,917 sq. mi.** (587,713 km²) in area, is Africa's biggest island and the fourth largest in the world. It is home to 200,000 known species of wildlife, many of them existing nowhere else in the world • Africa's mega wildlife reserve is the **13,513 sq. mi.** (35,000 km²) Great Limpopo Transfrontier Park, linking South Africa, Mozambique, and Zimbabwe • The southernmost of Africa's Great Lakes is called Malawi (Nyasa) and is said to have more **species of fish** than any other lake in the world.

HOT MEETS COLD
Where cold ocean currents meet the Namib Desert, banks of fog roll in over the dunes.

?

WHO OR WHAT AM I?
I am superhard, sparkly—and can be worth a million dollars.

ANSWER: A diamond

WHO LIVES HERE?

The oldest inhabitants of this region are the **Khoi-San** peoples. Hundreds of other African peoples live here, such as the **Herero, Tswana, Ndebele, Shona, Zulu,** and **Xhosa**. In South Africa there are also white **Afrikaners** and other people of **European** or **Asian** descent.

High flying! Kids from **Soweto, Johannesburg,** make the most of the swings.

The heaviest recorded white rhinoceros weighed **about 5 tons**.

SKIPPING IN SOWETO

Almost a million people live in the huge district of Soweto, near Johannesburg. In South Africa 30 years ago, black people and white people were not allowed to live in the same parts of town. The children of Soweto protested. All of that has changed today. Soweto has improved and is a lively place for music, dance, soccer, and street fashion.

A **braai** is a Southern African **barbecue**. It might include steaks, all kinds of sausages, ribs, chicken, or seafood.

Madagascar grows scented yellow flowers called **ylang-ylang**. They are used to prepare an oil used in making perfumes.

"HELLO" IN THE ZULU LANGUAGE:
Sawubona

DURBAN STREET FOOD:
"Bunny chow" (scooped-out loaf filled with curry)

ANCIENT STONES:
Great Zimbabwe, 800-year-old stone city

WORLD'S BIGGEST DIAMOND MINE:
(By area) Orapa, Botswana

PEBBLE PLANTS:
Clever camouflage—lithops plants look just like real stones

HIGH JUMPER:
The springbok (a kind of antelope) can leap 13 ft. (4 m) into the air

VANISHING RIVER:
Unlike most other rivers, the Okavango evaporates before it can reach the sea

Species of **lemur** are found only on **Madagascar**. The smallest of these furry animals weighs only **1 oz.** (30 g), but the biggest can weigh almost **20 lb.** (9 kg). Some of them come out only at night—and did you know that their name actually means "ghost"?

South Africa makes its money by mining precious diamonds and gold.

The world's **deepest** gold mine is at Mponeng, in South Africa. It burrows underground for more than **2 mi. (4 km).**

Jewelry dating back about **75,000 years** was found in the **Blombos Cave, South Africa**.

The beads were made of snail shells.

PHILIPPINE SEA

PALAU

FEDERATED STATES OF MICRONESIA

MARSHALL ISLANDS (U.

PAPUA NEW GUINEA

SOLOMON ISLANDS

MELANESIA

NEW CALEDONIA (FRANCE)

VANUATU

FIJI

Northern Territory

Queensland

Western Australia

AUSTRALIA

South Australia

New South Wales

Victoria

Tasmania

NEW ZEALAND

North Island

TASMAN SEA

South Island

MAP KEY
1 Shipwreck Galleries 2 Kangaroo
3 Purnululu National Park 4 Jellyfish
5 Great Barrier Reef 6 Koala bear 7 Uluru
8 Eucalyptus 9 Sydney Opera House
10 Kiwi 11 Easter Island statue

Area: 3 300,000 sq. mi. (8,600,000 km²)
Fact: Smallest continent
Population: 37 million in 2013

Oceania straddles 10 different time zones. This means that if it's 9:00 A.M. on Easter Island, the easternmost end of the continent, in Palau, on the western side, it will still be midnight. Way too early to get up!

SOUTHERN OCEAN

Oceania

"Aim for the highest cloud so that if you miss it, you will hit a lofty mountain."

Maori proverb

EQUATOR

MICRONESIA

PHOENIX ISLANDS

TOKELAU

SOCIETY ISLANDS

SAMOA

TROPIC
OF CAPRICORN

COOK ISLANDS

TUAMOTU ISLANDS

TONGA

11

POLYNESIA

PACIFIC OCEAN

EASTER ISLAND

The continent of Oceania is full of strange and fascinating landscapes, unusual plants and animals, and ancient myths and legends. It's the smallest continent in the world.

Oceania also has the second-smallest population of all continents. People who have lived here since before written language began to share their world with European newbies, who've only been here a few hundred years. Many of the plants and animals native to Oceania are not found naturally anywhere else in the world. And some of them are very odd looking!

A lot of Oceania is desert, but there are also rain forests, volcanoes, and dry grasslands. Many of its islands are volcanic or coral islands, and some are covered in mountains and forests. Some of the landscapes of Oceania look almost as though they belong to another planet, and the locals keep alive myths and legends explaining why they're there. With mushrooms that throw their hats at you, mammals with pouches, and trees that look as though they're growing upside down, Oceania is an astonishing place.

Oceania

Oceania really is an island continent. In fact, it contains about 25,000 islands, spread over an area of ocean larger than the all of Asia. Most of them are very small and are the tops of underwater mountains. Only a few thousand are inhabited. Many Pacific Islanders lead traditional lives, fishing and farming for food, trading between islands on their wooden sailboats, and living in houses thatched with palm fronds. However, there are also more modern industries, such as mining and tourism, which provide employment for large numbers of people.

The length of **Australia's eastern coastline** is **4,285 mi.** (6,853 km)

RAINBOW BEE-EATER, PAPUA NEW GUINEA

GREAT BARRIER REEF

FOX GLACIER, NEW ZEALAND

POUAKAI RANGE, EGMONT NATIONAL PARK, NEW ZEALAND

Superlative Oceania

In the Southern Hemisphere, where Oceania is, June, July, and August are the winter months, and December, January, and February are the summer • Oceania includes Australia, New Zealand (although it is not on the same continental shelf), New Guinea, Tasmania, and thousands of smaller islands • The continent straddles the International Date Line, which means that children in some countries will be complaining about having to go to school on Monday while others practically next door are still asleep after a relaxing Sunday! That's so not fair!

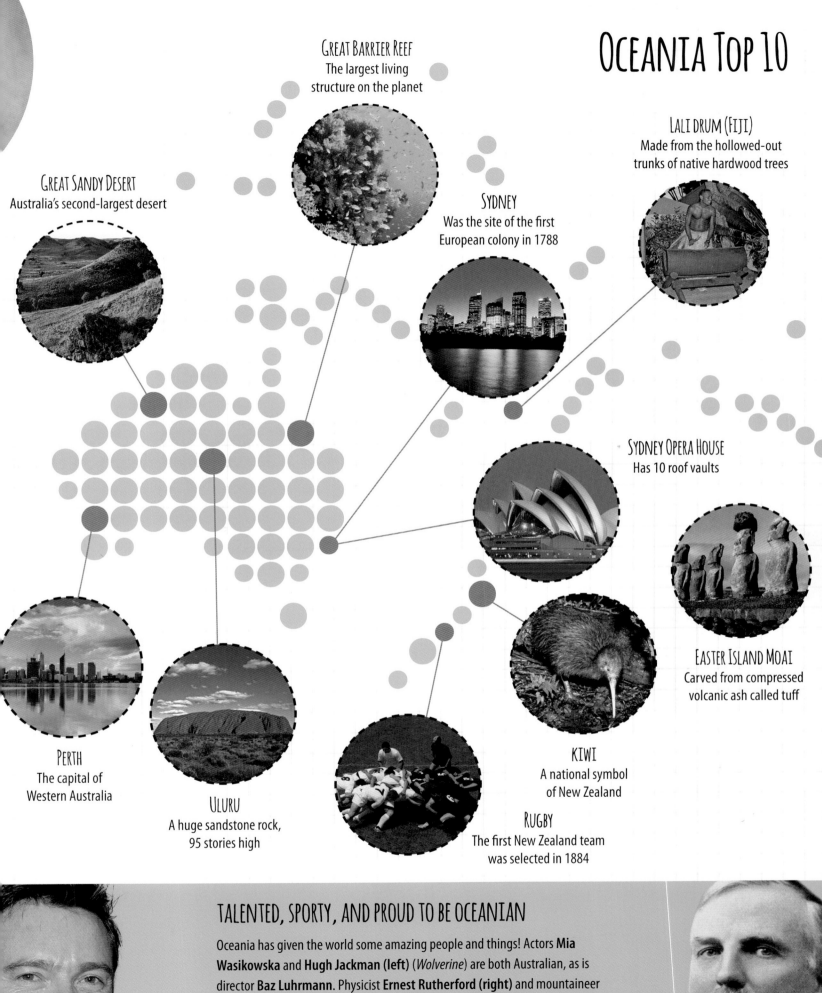

OCEANIA TOP 10

GREAT BARRIER REEF
The largest living structure on the planet

LALI DRUM (FIJI)
Made from the hollowed-out trunks of native hardwood trees

GREAT SANDY DESERT
Australia's second-largest desert

SYDNEY
Was the site of the first European colony in 1788

SYDNEY OPERA HOUSE
Has 10 roof vaults

EASTER ISLAND MOAI
Carved from compressed volcanic ash called tuff

PERTH
The capital of Western Australia

ULURU
A huge sandstone rock, 95 stories high

RUGBY
The first New Zealand team was selected in 1884

KIWI
A national symbol of New Zealand

TALENTED, SPORTY, AND PROUD TO BE OCEANIAN

Oceania has given the world some amazing people and things! Actors **Mia Wasikowska** and **Hugh Jackman (left)** (*Wolverine*) are both Australian, as is director **Baz Luhrmann**. Physicist **Ernest Rutherford (right)** and mountaineer **Edmund Hillary** were both New Zealanders, and **Ricky Ponting**, former Australian cricket team member, and **Mary Donaldson**, Crown Princess of Denmark, are Tasmanian——as is **Taz**, the famous cartoon Tasmanian devil.

Australia and Papua New Guinea

The enormous country of Australia is famous for its unusual wildlife, including marsupials (mammals with pouches), such as kangaroos and wallabies, and the enormous emu, a flightless bird. Its people are famous for being tough and outdoorsy; sports and barbecues on the beach are among Australians' favorite leisure activities! Papua New Guinea takes up the eastern half of the island of New Guinea, as well as other smaller islands. Spanish and Portuguese explorers found the islands in the 1500s. The name Papua was chosen by a Portuguese explorer and is a Malay word for frizzy hair. Later, a Spanish explorer named the island New Guinea because its people reminded him of those from African Guinea.

THREE SISTERS, BLUE MOUNTAINS

WAVE ROCK, AUSTRALIA

PERTH

GREAT BARRIER REEF SO LARGE IT CAN BE SEEN FROM SPACE

SYDNEY OPERA HOUSE

PAPUA
NEW GUINEA

PORT MORESBY

DARWIN

CAIRNS

Tanami Desert

Great Sandy Desert

AUSTRALIA   Simpson Desert

Gibson Desert

BRISBANE

Great Victoria Desert

SYDNEY

CANBERRA

SYDNEY SKYLINE

MELBOURNE

Tasmania

TASMAN
SEA

PAPUA NEW GUINEA TRADITIONAL DRESS

EMU, SECOND-LARGEST BIRD IN THE WORLD AFTER THE OSTRICH

PACIFIC
OCEAN

SUPER STATS

Sydney is the **largest city** in Australia and is the home of the Sydney Opera House and Sydney Harbour Bridge. The bridge is the widest single-span bridge in the world, at an enormous **161 ft. (49 m)**! • New Guinea is the second-largest island in the world (Greenland is the biggest, unless you count Australia itself, which is officially a continent, not an island) • People have lived here for about **50,000** years, and today there are about **850** different languages and cultures • The **smallest town** in Australia (Cooladdi, Queensland) has a motel, train station, and four-star restaurant—but only four people live there!

ABORIGINAL ART

Traditional arts and crafts in Australia include painting on leaves, wood and bark carving, rock carving, sculpture, making ceremonial clothing, jewelry making, basket weaving, cave painting, and sand painting. Much of the art tells a story from the ancient myths and legends of the people. If the story is an important or secret one, only an artist whose family "owns" the story can paint it.

?

WHO AM I?

I'm a great tree climber and just LOVE eating eucalyptus. Think I'm cute? Watch my bite!

ANSWER: Koala

ABORIGINAL PAINTING

WHO LIVES HERE?

The original Australians are the **Aboriginals**, descendants of **Asian** people. The majority of Australians nowadays, however, are the descendants of Europeans who colonized the land in the **1700s** or are very recent arrivals. Papua New Guinea's people are mostly Melanesian, Papuan, Negrito, Micronesian, and Polynesian.

14,793 ft. (4,509 m) above sea level, **Mount Wilhelm** is the highest point in Papua New Guinea—and in all of Oceania!

Papua New Guinea is close to the **equator** and is very warm. Yet on Mount Wilhelm and other high places, it sometimes has **snow!**

SING-SING SENSATION

Around Papua New Guinea's Independence Day (September 16), Sing-Sings take place across the country. These festivals are amazing sights with more than 100 tribes showing off their music, dance, and culture. You can see painted warriors with feathered headdresses dancing to the beat of the Kundu drums, while the mud men of Asaro look very fierce!

20% of Australia's total population lives in Sydney!

WHAT TO SAY:
Beaut, beudy, bonzer, ripper (they all mean "good" in Australian English)

WHAT NOT TO SAY:
Why don't you have corks on your hat?

FAMOUS FOR:
Tough, outdoor types

INFAMOUS FOR:
Ned Kelly

DANGEROUS ANIMALS:
Lots! Sharks, poisonous spiders and snakes, kangaroos . . .

SPORTS:
Australian football, surfing

JOB:
Bush ranger

HOBBY:
Going walkabout

FOOD:
Meat pies, Vegemite

6,500 people speak Auslan, a sign language for deaf people. Here's how to say "Auslan" in Auslan!

400
Australian Aboriginal languages existed when Europeans first arrived.

Only about **70** are still spoken, and about 40 of those are endangered.

One of the world's only known poisonous bird, the **hooded pitohul,** is native to Papua New Guinea.

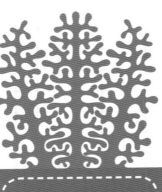

At **1,243 mi. (2,000 km),** the **Great Barrier Reef** is the longest coral reef in the world.

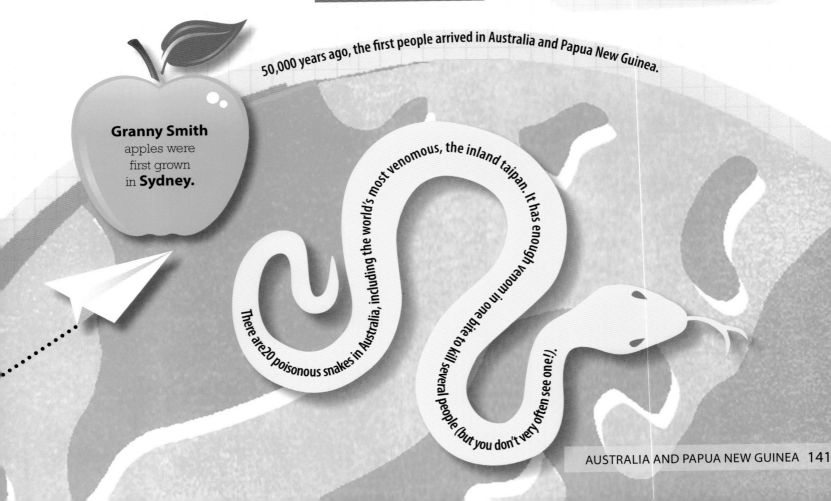

50,000 years ago, the first people arrived in Australia and Papua New Guinea.

Granny Smith apples were first grown in **Sydney.**

There are 20 poisonous snakes in Australia, including the world's most venomous, the inland taipan. It has enough venom in one bite to kill several people (but you don't very often see one!).

New Zealand and the Pacific Islands

New Zealand is a group of mountainous islands in the Pacific Ocean. The landscape is beautiful and varied, including volcanoes, snowy peaks, rocky shores, and lush green fields. The only mammals to have reached the place without human help are bats, so birds and insects occupy what would normally be the place of mammals elsewhere. With few natural enemies, many birds, such as kiwis and moas, have lost the ability to fly. The New Zealand people are a mixed bunch, and languages spoken include Samoan, French, Hindi, and Chinese. But they all love their sports, especially rugby and cricket. While the far north of New Zealand has subtropical weather during the summer, and the south can get really cold in the winter, most of the country lies close to the coast, which means temperatures are mild. The Pacific Islands mostly have a tropical climate.

FEDERATED STATES OF MICRONESIA

PALAU

SOLOMON ISLANDS

THE BORA BORA LAGOON

SNOW-CAPPED PEAK
Mount Taranaki showing western flanks of dormant volcano above clouds, New Zealand.

CORAL REEF, FIJI

MAORI WOOD CARVING

MARSHALL ISLANDS (U.S.)

EQUATOR

MICRONESIA

MOUNT COOK

MELANESIA

PHOENIX ISLANDS

SOCIETY ISLANDS

VANUATU

SAMOAN ISLANDS

COOK ISLANDS

FIJI

TUAMOTU ISLANDS

NEW CALEDONIA (FRANCE)

TONGA

POLYNESIA

PACIFIC OCEAN

NORTH ISLAND

AUCKLAND

KIWI

EASTER ISLAND

NEW ZEALAND

WELLINGTON

CHRISTCHURCH

DUNEDIN

SOUTH ISLAND

EASTER ISLAND STATUES

AUCKLAND SKY TOWER, NEW ZEALAND

SUPER STATS

The Auckland Sky Tower opened in 1997 and is the tallest freestanding structure in the Southern Hemisphere, at **1,076 ft. (328 m)** • Taveuni Island in Fiji is crossed by the International Date Line, allowing you to put one foot in today and one in yesterday! • Bungee jumping originated on Vanuatu with the inhabitants tying vines around their ankles and thowing themselves off a high tower.

MYSTERIOUS MOAI

Easter Island is home to almost 900 huge carved statues known as moai. On average, they stand 13 ft. (4 m) high and weigh 13 tons. But the reason why these enormous stone figures were created remains a mystery.

143

WHO LIVES HERE?

The first people to arrive here were the **Maoris**, in about the A.D. 1200s. They named the country **Aotearoa**, which means "The land of the long white cloud." Dutch geographers gave it the name **Nieuw Zeeland**, after a region of the Netherlands. After James Cook sailed here in 1769, the British settled it and signed a treaty with more than **500 Maori chiefs** from tribes throughout the country. It seems the English version of the treaty said that the Queen of England was now to rule the country, and the Maori version said that the Maoris were. The debate still rages about who should really be in control! Whatever the answer, New Zealand still attracts plenty of international immigrants, especially from nearby Asian countries.

New Zealand was the first country to give all **women** the right to vote, in **1893**.

The national day in New Zealand is **Waitangi Day**, on February 6. It's the day that the treaty between the British and Maori peoples was signed. Many local communities run events during the day, including kapa haka, the cultural dance of the Maoris.

EXPLORING ROTORUA

Rotorua in the Bay of Plenty region of New Zealand's North Island is one very smelly place! The stench, like rotten eggs, comes from sulfur in its many gushing geysers, hot springs, and hissing mud pools. Here you'll find Hell's Gate (Tikitere), the largest hot waterfall in the Southern Hemisphere. Truly amazing!

THE OCEANIA REAL DEAL!

WHAT TO SAY:
Kia ora ("hello" in Maori language)

FAMOUS FOR:
Ernest Rutherford, the first man to split the atom, in 1919

INFAMOUS FOR:
Bungee jumping (the first commercial bungee jump in the world was a 141 ft. (43 m) leap off Kawarau Bridge in Queenstown in 1988)

ANIMALS:
The world's smallest marine dolphin, the Hector's dolphin, which grows to a maximum of 5 ft. (1.5 m) long, is found only in the waters off New Zealand

SNAKES:
None. Not one. Not in New Zealand

FOOD:
Green-lipped mussels, supposed to be good for arthritis sufferers!

FESTIVAL:
Waitangi Day

86% of New Zealand's population lives in cities. Once, the vast majority were farmers.

25% of the world's volcanoes are in the Pacific Ring of Fire.

New Zealand has more **golf** courses per person than any other country!

Rugby is the most popular sport in New Zealand, and almost everyone is a big fan of the national team, the **All Blacks.**

23 million years ago, New Zealand's islands first appeared, pushed up out of the ocean by volcanic activity.

New Zealanders are often known as **"kiwis,"** after the bird.

2.5 oz. (70 g)
The giant weta, one of the world's heaviest insects, lives in New Zealand.

New Zealand exports lots of lamb, butter and wine. Tourism and fishing are also important for the economy.

12,316 ft. (3,754 m)
Mount Cook is the highest peak in New Zealand. The Maoris call it "Cloud Piercer."

2 million tourists a year visit **New Zealand.** Tourism is the country's biggest industry.

Antarctica

"... the only place on earth that is still as it should be. May we never tame it."

Andrew Denton

Antarctica's landscape is barren, but beautiful. There are hardly any plants or animals on the land even in the summer, and in the winter only male penguins stay there, taking care of their eggs while the females go off to feed. No people live here permanently, but there are scientific research bases, and researchers stay from three months to about two years to work. The only other people are visitors to the bases, tourists, and explorers.

Antarctica is the only one of the continents to be permanently covered in ice and snow. It's also the windiest continent. Blizzards, like sandstorms in hot deserts, pick up snow and whirl it around so that it's almost impossible to see. There are no trees or bushes, only simple plants such as mosses, lichen, and algae, and the occasional small flower in the summer! Penguins, seals, whales, fish, and krill live in the waters around Antarctica.

SOUTH ATLANTIC OCEAN

Antarctic Peninsula

Palmer Land

Ellsworth Land

SOUTH PACIFIC OCEAN

There is so much ice in Antarctica that the weight of the ice sheets is pushing the land beneath them into the Earth. If all of the ice melted, the land would rise about 1,625 ft. (500 m). But it would take 10,000 years!

Area: 5.5 million sq. mi. (14 million km²)
Fact: Fifth-largest continent
Population in the summer: About 4,000 scientists
Population in the winter: About 1,000 scientists

MAP KEY
1 Squid 2 Fur seal 3 Leopard seal 4 Research stations from around the world are dotted all over 5 Antarctic pearlwort 6 Emperor penguin 7 Elephant seal 8 McMurdo research station 9 Minke whale 10 The ceremonial South Pole

WEDDELL
SEA

Queen Maud Land

Enderby Land

Kemp
Land

Ronne
Ice Shelf

Princess Elizabeth
Land

Polar Plateau

East Antarctica

Kaiser Wilhelm II
Land

West Antarctica

Transantarctic Ridge

Queen Mary Land

Ross
Ice Shelf

Marie Byrd Land

Wilkes Land

Victoria Land

INDIAN
OCEAN

ANTARCTICA

Scientists working at the research bases here carry out a wide range of work! Studies include how the human body and mind adapt to cold conditions. Researchers also drill ice cores to try to figure out the history of the continent, and they study penguins, fish, global warming, glaciology, astronomy, and climatology. It's also a great spot to search for meteorites— the dark rocks stand out against the snow!

GERMAN ANTARCTIC RESEARCH BASE

Antarctica was the last of the continents to be discovered—probably in **1820,** when American seal hunter John Davis said he landed on it.

−129.27°F (−89.6°C) The lowest temperature ever recorded, at the Russian Vostok Station in Antarctica.

HISTORIC EXPLORERS Norwegian Roald Amundsen and his team were the first explorers to reach the South Pole, in 1912.

2 in. (50 mm) of precipitation per year. Nearly all of it falls as snow.

Sunrise at the South Pole happens around September 21 every year. Sunset is happens around March 21 the following year.

POLAR OPPOSITES

While Antarctica is a continent, or landmass, its opposite in the north, the Arctic, is a huge frozen ocean surrounded by land belonging to many different countries. For much of the year, the arctic ice is so thick that animals and people can walk on it just as if it were land.

THE EMPEROR PENGUIN, THE BIGGEST IN THE WORLD AT OVER 3 FT. (1 M) TALL, LIVES ON ANTARCTICA.

DEEP FREEZE

The ice of Antarctica is not a solid sheet. Glaciers are constantly on the move, breaking the ice and forming huge crevasses (cracks). Icebergs form along the coast, where ice shelves and glaciers break off and fall into the ocean.

ELEPHANT SEAL

87% of all the **ice** on the planet is found in **Antarctica.**

WHAT TO WEAR

Because of the cold and wind, people going outside in the Antarctic usually wear several layers of clothing—a soft, breathable one next to the skin that will wick away perspiration while they're working, then two or three insulating layers that they can take off if they get really warm. Two pairs of socks and gloves are also pretty crucial!

SUPER STATS

4,247 sq. mi. (11,000km²) above water (and ten times as big below), the largest iceberg recorded broke off from the Ross Ice Shelf in 2000 • On Deception Island, off the Antarctic Peninsula, people bathe in warm water heated by a volcano while surrounded by ice! • Lake Vostok, a liquid lake deep below the surface of Antarctica, may contain signs of life. Scientists are busy drilling down about **13,000 ft.** (4,000 m) to reach it and find out • Mount Erebus is the world's southernmost active volcano and Antarctica's highest mountain, at **12,447 ft.** (3,794 m).

In 1961 the **Antarctic Treaty** was signed, controlling human activity in the region. Countries that have signed the treaty are free to carry out **scientific experiments** but must **conserve** the environment.

?

WHO OR WHAT AM I?

I come to Antarctica to breed. I have a 10 ft. (3 m) wingspan and I can live for over 60 years. Also, I'm famous for protecting sailors.

ANSWER: An albatross

World quiz

1. In which country is the **Great Pyramid of Giza** located?

....

2. What is the **largest land mammal** on the planet?

a) Elephant
b) Blue whale
c) Nile crocodile

3. What is the **largest mammal** on the planet?

a) Elephant
b) Blue whale
c) Koala

4. What are the colors of the **French flag**?

....

5. **Aboriginal Australians** believe that there was a time when animal, plant, and human ancestors created the world and everything it contains. What is this time called?

....

6. In Ethiopia, **how many months** are there in a year?

....

7. To the **east and west of Africa** are two oceans. Which two are they?

....

8. What is the **largest hot desert** in the world, and on which continent is it found?

....

9. What is the capital of **Egypt**?

a) Nairobi
b) Cayenne
c) Cairo

10. What are the colors of the **Chadian flag**?

....

11. What is the easternmost point of the **African continent** called?

a) Leg of Africa
b) Toe of Africa
c) Horn of Africa

12. Which is the **tallest** animal in the world?

a) Ostrich
b) Giraffe
c) Emu

13. What is the **largest country** in Africa?

a) Republic of Congo
b) Algeria
c) Rwanda

14. What was the **lowest temperature** ever recorded?

a) −49.35°F (−45.2°C)
b) −129.27°F (−89.6°C)
c) −215.85°F (−137.7°C)

15. How many different kinds of **ants** are there?

a) More than 14,000

b) Fewer than 5,000

c) More than 100,000

16. **Worker ants** are all female. **True or false**?

....

17. The **Yangtze** is the longest river in the world. **True or false**?

....

18. **Tropical rain forests** are cold and wet. **True or false**?

....

19. **Indonesian people** grow their staple food, rice, on terraces. **True or false**?

....

20. What are the colors of the **Italian flag**?

....

21. Our planet, **Earth**, is the closest planet to the Sun. **True or false**?

....

22. What is the interior region of **Australia** called?

a) The inside

b) The outdoors

c) The outback

23. How many **saunas** are there in Finland?

a) 20,000

b) 200,000

c) 2 million

24. What is the capital of **Australia**?

....

25. In which **country** are the states of Queensland and Victoria?

....

26. The **Aztecs** were an ancient people in which modern country?

....

27. What is a **bridge** that carries water called?

....

28. **Camels and llamas** are closely related. What does a camel have that a llama does not?

....

29. **Canada** is the second-largest country in the world. **True or false**?

....

30. The **Caribbean** islands are also sometimes called the West Indies. **True or false**?

....

31. **Climate** is short term, weather is long term. **True or false**?

....

32. Which is the **largest** continent?

....

33. The **tectonic plates** carrying the continents move at about the rate of 1 in. (1.5 cm) per year. **True or false**?

....

34. Where do most **earthquakes** happen?

a) Close to the edges of the tectonic plates
b) In hot countries
c) In cool countries

35. How many different **kinds of elephants** are there?

....

36. **Catfish** are covered in large scales. **True or false**?

....

37. What can **flying squirrels** do?

a) Fly
b) Jump
c) Glide

38. How many **legs** do insects have?

a) 8
b) 12
c) 6

39. What shape is an **Australian football** field?

....

40. What is the capital of **Germany**?

....

41. Approximately what percentage of an **iceberg** is underwater?

....

42. What continent does the **rhea** inhabit?

....

43. What is the capital of **India**?

....

44. In which country were **Lego** bricks first made?

....

45. How many kinds of **camels** are there?

....

46. How many humps does a **dromedary camel** have?

....

47. What is the capital of **Luxembourg**?

....

48. Which island of **New Zealand** contains its capital, Wellington?

....

49. Which **ocean** is the largest and deepest?

....

50. What is the main cause of **ocean tides**?

....

51. What is the world's largest **invertebrate**?

....

52. Where did the first **Olympic Games** take place?

a) Italy
b) France
c) Greece

53. What is the world's **biggest** living bird?

a) The ostrich
b) The emu
c) The cassowary

54. What are the colors of the **Jamaican flag**?

....

55. **Ostriches and emus** can neither fly nor swim. **True or false**?

....

56. What color are a **cassowary's eggs**?

....

57. About how many **Pacific islands** are there?

a) 5000
b) 15,000
c) 25,000

58. Which country is home to **pizza, pasta** and **gelato**?

a) Italy
b) Burundi
c) Australia

59. What **sweet treat** is made from the cacao bean?

....

60. What is the **largest lizard** in the world?

....

61. In which country would you find the **Taj Mahal**?

....

62. Which country is the world's largest exporter of **false teeth**?

....

63. Which was the **last continent** to be discovered?

....

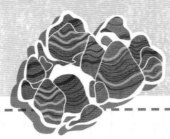

64. How many tons was the **heaviest** white rhino ever to be recorded?

a) 0.5

b) 2

c) 5

65. Which country owns the **Faeroe Islands**?

. . . .

66. Which two oceans does the **Panama Canal** connect?

. . . .

67. What do **sharks and rays** have where most other fish have bones?

a) Cartilage

b) Muscle

c) Teeth

68. Of which country was **Robert Bruce** once king?

a) Australia

b) Scotland

c) Ireland

69. Which country is famous for **flamenco music** and dance?

. . . .

70. What is the **biggest fish** in the sea?

. . . .

71. Which is the **longest river** in South America?

a) The Andes

b) The Aymara

c) The Amazon

72. On which continent would you find the cities of **Caracas, Bogotà, and Brasilia**?

a) Europe

b) South America

c) North America

73. In which country is **Rio de Janeiro**?

a) Brazil

b) Spain

c) Bolivia

74. In which country is the island of **Java**?

. . . .

75. Where can you find the beautiful Moorish **Alhambra palace**?

a) North Africa

b) South Africa

c) Spain

76. How many legs does a **spider** have?

. . . .

77. What are the colors of the **Japanese flag**?

. . . .

78. How many points are there on the **Statue of Liberty's crown**?

a) 6
b) 7
c) 8

79. What was the last state to join the **United States of America**?

. . . .

80. How many **states** are there in the United States?

a) 10
b) 50
c) 100

81. From which **three countries** did the Vikings originate?

. . . .

82. There are fewer than **200 active volcanoes** in the world. **True or false**?

. . . .

ANSWERS

1) Egypt
2) A
3) B
4) Red, white, and blue
5) Dreamtime
6) 13
7) The Atlantic Ocean and the Indian Ocean
8) The Sahara, in Africa, at more than 3.3 million sq. mi.
9) C (9.4 million km²)
10) Blue, yellow, and red
11) C
12) B
13) B
14) B
15) A
16) True
17) False. The longest river is the Nile, in Africa, at 4,159 mi. (6,693 km)
18) False. Tropical rain forests are hot and wet
19) True

20) Green, white, and red
21) False. Mercury is the closest planet to the Sun. Earth is third closest
22) C
23) C
24) Canberra
25) Australia
26) Mexico
27) An aqueduct
28) A hump (or two)
29) True
30) True
31) False. Weather is short term, and climate is long term
32) Asia
33) True
34) A
35) Two; the African and the Asian elephant
36) False. Catfish are smooth-skinned.
37) C
38) C
39) Oval

40) Berlin
41) 90
42) South America
43) New Delhi
44) Denmark
45) Two; dromedary and Bactrian
46) One
47) Luxembourg
48) North Island
49) The Pacific
50) The gravity of the Moon
51) The giant squid
52) C
53) A
54) Green, gold, and black
55) False. They can swim, but they can't fly
56) Green
57) C
58) A
59) Chocolate
60) The Komodo dragon
61) India
62) Liechtenstein
63) Antarctica

64) C
65) Denmark
66) The Pacific Ocean and the Atlantic Ocean
67) A
68) B
69) Spain
70) The whale shark
71) C
72) B
73) A
74) Indonesia
75) C
76) Eight
77) White and red
78) B
79) Hawaii
80) B
81) Norway, Sweden, and Denmark
82) False. There are more than 1,500 potentially active volcanoes, and at least 500 of them have erupted in recorded history

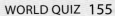

Index map

If you want to find a particular place shown on this map, you can look for it in the index on pages 158–159. Its grid reference (a letter followed by a number, like "H5") will help you pinpoint exactly where on this map it is located.

	A	B	C	D	E	F	G
1							
2						Greenland (Denmark)	GREENL. SEA
3		BEAUFORT SEA		BAFFIN BAY			
4	BERING SEA	Alaska (USA)	Canada	Hudson Bay / Davis Strait		Iceland	Northern Ireland U. / Ireland E.
5		Gulf of Alaska	NORTH AMERICA		NORTH ATLANTIC OCEAN		Portugal
6	NORTH PACIFIC OCEAN	Hawaii (USA)	Mexico / GULF OF MEXICO / Cuba / Bahamas	Turks & Caicos Islands (UK) / Puerto Rico (USA) / Dominican Republic / Haiti / Cayman Islands / Belize / Honduras / Jamaica / Guatemala / El Salvador / Nicaragua / CARIBBEAN SEA / St Kitts & Nevis / Antigua & Barbuda / Dominica / St Lucia / Barbados / St Vincent & the Grenadines	Bermuda (UK)	Madeira (Portugal) / Canary Islands (Spain) / Cape Verde / Gambia / Guinea-Bissau / Western Sahara / Mauritania / Senegal / Guinea / Sierra Leone / Liberia	Moro.
7	Kiribati / OCEANIA / Samoa	French Polynesia (France)	Galápagos Islands (Ecuador)	Costa Rica / Panama / Colombia / Ecuador / Venezuela / Guyana / Suriname / French Guiana / Trinidad & Tobago / Peru / Bolivia	Brazil / SOUTH AMERICA		
8	Fiji / Tonga		Easter Island (Chile)	Paraguay / Argentina / Uruguay / Chile	SOUTH ATLANTIC OCEAN		
9	SOUTH PACIFIC OCEAN			Falkland Islands (UK) / Scotia Sea	South Georgia (UK)		
10					South Orkney Islands (Antartica)		
11	ROSS SEA			Antarctica	WEDDELL SEA		

SOUTHERN OCEAN

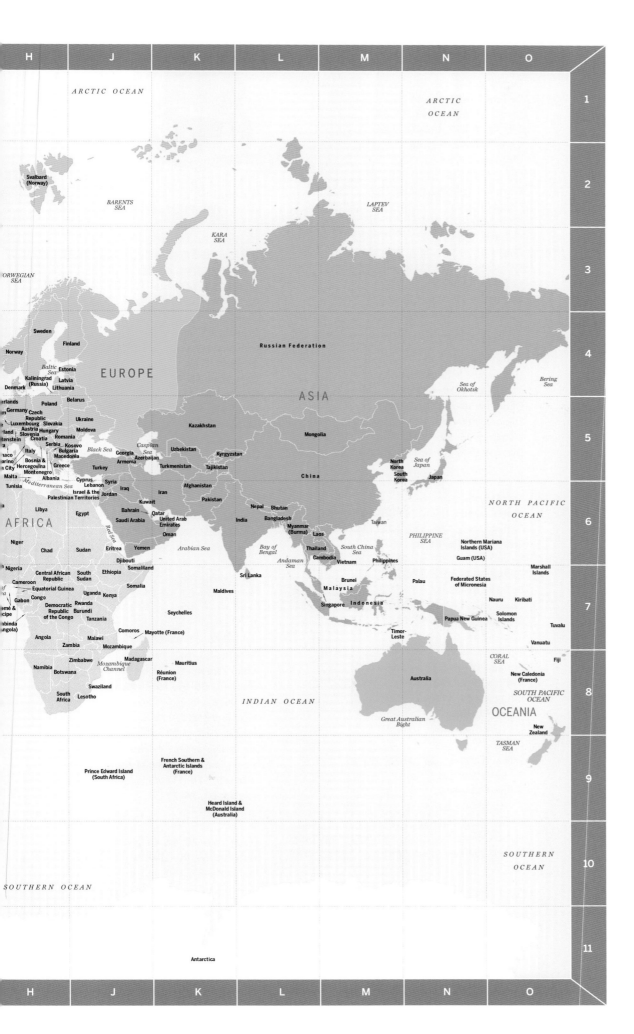

Index

Acknowledgments

Published in October 2014 by Lonely Planet Publications Pty Ltd

ABN 36 005 607 983
www.lonelyplanet.com
ISBN 978 1 74360 433 5
© Lonely Planet 2014
© Photographs as indicated 2014
Printed in China

Publishing Director	Piers Pickard
Publisher	Mina Patria
Art Director	Beverley Speight
Project Manager	Jessica Cole
Authors	Deborah Murrell, Philip Steele
Illustrator	Alice Lickens
Layout Designers	Kevin Knight, Lisa McCormick
Image Researcher	Shweta Andrews
Cartography	Wayne Murphy, Anita Banh, Corey Hutchinson
Pre-press production	Tag Response
Print production	Larissa Frost

Thanks to Joe Bindloss, Jo Cooke, Laura Crawford, Megan Eaves, Helen Elfer, Lisa Eyre, Sue Grabham, Gemma Graham, Alex Howard, Kate Morgan, MaSovaida Morgan, Matt Phillips, Dee Pilgrim, Sarah Reid, James Smart, Dan Tucker, Anna Tyler, Branislava Vladisavljevic, Tasmin Waby, Dora Whitaker, Clifton Wilkinson

PHOTO CREDITS

KEY: t -top, tc-top center, tr-top right, tl-top left, tcr- top center right, tcl- top center left, c-center, cr-center right, cl-center left, ca-center above, cb-center below, cla-center left above, cra-center right above, clb- center left below, crb – center right below, b-bottom, bc-bottom center, br-bottom right, bl-bottom left, bg-background.

Corbis: 11tc, 29bl, 63t, 80c, 91br, 96, 102 – 103c, 102bg, 127br, 139tr, 142bg, 142bl, 143cb, 148tr, 148cr, 149cr.

Getty Images: 11cl, 11crb, 18b, 19t, 19c, 28bg, 28t, 29tc, 29tr, 29cra, 29crb, 29cb, 29clb, 29cl, 29tl, 29tcl, 30t, 40, 42cr, 43tr, 43c, 43cl, 44, 48bg, 48tr, 48cra, 48c, 48clb, 49tr, 49cr, 49crb, 49c, 49cb, 49clb, 49cl, 49cla, 49tl, 49bl, 50cr, 50bg, 51tr, 51crb, 52, 54bg, 55cl, 56, 60bg, 60tr, 60cra, 60c, 60bc, 61tc, 61tr, 61cr, 61crb, 61cb, 61clb, 61cl, 61cla, 61tl, 62t, 62cr, 62bg, 62bl, 63br, 64, 64cb, 66tr, 66cr, 66crb, 66bg, 66bl, 67crb, 68, 70bl, 70 – 71bg, 70 – 71b, 71tr, 71cr, 71cl, 72, 74tr, 74cr, 74bg, 75tr, 75br, 75bc, 76, 76c, 78tr, 78cr, 78 – 79bg, 78bl, 79br, 80, 81clb, 82tr, 82cr, 82bg, 83tr, 83cr, 83bc, 84, 88bg, 88tc, 88crb, 88br, 89tc, 89tr, 89cra, 89cr, 89crb, 89cb, 89clb, 89cl, 89tl, 89bl, 90cr, 90bg, 91c, 92, 94tr, 94cr, 94bg, 94bl, 95tr, 95cr, 98tr, 98cr, 98bg, 98bl, 99cr, 99bc, 100, 102tr, 103tr, 103br, 104, 106tl, 106cl, 107tl, 108, 110tr, 110bl, 111tr, 111crb, 111bc, 112, 116bg, 116br, 118tr, 118cr, 118br, 118bc, 119cl, 119br, 120, 122cr, 122bg, 122cl, 123cra, 124, 126cr, 126, 127tr, 127cl, 128, 130cr, 130bl, 131crb, 131c, 132, 136bg, 136tr, 136cra, 136br, 137tc, 137tr, 137ca, 137cra, 137cr, 137crb, 137cb, 137clb, 137cl, 137tl, 138tr, 138cr, 138br, 138bg, 139br, 140, 142cr, 143bc, 144, 148 – 149bg, 149cl.

Indiapicture: 29br, 49tc, 49br, 61br, 61bl, 82bl, 84c, 88ca, 89br, 102bl, 117bl, 117br, 137br, 137bl.

iStock: 6c, 8cr, 13tl, 13tr, 13cra, 13cb, 13clb, 15br, 16bcl, 16bcr, 19b, 20b, 28cr, 28b, 28clb, 30bg, 30bl, 30crb, 31crb, 32, 34cla, 34crb, 34bg, 35tr, 35br, 35bc, 36, 37c, 37cr, 38tr, 38cr, 38bg, 39tc, 39cl, 39b, 42bg, 43cr, 43b, 48bl, 50tr, 50bl, 54tr, 54cr, 54br, 54bl, 74 – 75b, 90c, 105cl, 110bg, 116tr, 116ca, 116cr, 117tc, 117tr, 117cra, 117cr, 117crb, 117clb, 117cl, 117cla, 117tl, 118bg, 118bl, 119c, 122tr, 123br, 126bl, 130bg, 131tc, 136cr, 139c, 139clb, 142br, 143tr, 143crb, 152bc, 154bc.

National Aeronautics and Space Administration (NASA): 37cb.

Shutterstock: 33tl, 65cla, 70tr, 70tr, 93t, 110cr.

LONELY PLANET OFFICES

AUSTRALIA
90 Maribyrnong St, Footscray, Victoria, 3011, Australia
Phone 03 8379 8000 Email talk2us@lonelyplanet.com.au

USA
150 Linden St, Oakland, CA 94607
Phone 510 250 6400 Email info@lonelyplanet.com

UNITED KINGDOM
Media Centre, 201 Wood Lane, London W12 7TQ
Phone 020 8433 1333 Email go@lonelyplanet.co.uk

Paper in this book is certified against the Forest Stewardship Council™ standards. FSC™ promotes environmentally responsible, socially beneficial and economically viable management of the world's forests.